Maradona good, Pele better, GEORGE BEST

Pete McKenna

Eternal thanks to:

Carmen Del Castillo for keeping the dreams alive; to the delectable Michelle for all her hard work editing this story; to Jason Brummell for turning it into reality; the magnificent Grennell family for being there as always; Snowy, Matty, Ray and England's finest John King for their support and kindness.

To the talented artist Dinga Bell whose fine painting graces the cover of this book - please check his work on the ArtbyDingo Facebook page.

And finally to George Best who though his unique charisma and awesome talent changed football forever who once said "I spent thousands of pounds on booze birds and fast cars. The rest I just squandered." What a way to go!

Keep the Faith - Pete McKenna

Printed by Colour Five - www.colourfive.net

FOREWORD by Jason Brummell

Maradona good, Pele better, GEORGE BEST is a modern day odyssey. A journey that graces the pages as George once graced the hallowed turfs of football grounds; across the world in the sixties and seventies. It jinks and weaves its way into the penalty area of our consciousness, all the while hurdling the challenges of the demons that beset both Pete and George's life and that ultimately exacted the highest toll.

Pete's journey to Belfast to attend Best's funeral is also a parable for us all. Of the good bits when you're stood as the King of your domain, arm aloft, all inimitable grin and champagne eyes; when life is like the joyful promise of the beautiful game, beautifully realised. And of course, as is so often the case, the bad bits when the seemingly all-to-fleeting moments of greatness become the long hours of unhappiness, when some sink and others swim.

Pete sees both the looming self-destructive danger in the former, and the times when adversity defines us in the latter; and perhaps most befitting the subject his words lead us all on a merry dance before nestling victoriously into the far corner of the net of legacy. It tells us that we can all define the moments in life we wish to be remembered for.

www.suavecollective.co.uk

INTRODUCTION

I don't know about you but I get sick to the stomach whenever I hear the words 'celebrity culture.' A highly infectious virus, that's spread across the country from Land's End to John O'Groats responsible for warping the attitudes and aspirations of thousands of impressionable young kids to buy into the 'get rich quick' 'gimme-gimme' celebrity lifestyle, enjoyed by their squeaky clean designer idols whose posters adorn their bedroom walls, enticing their doting fans to strive to copy them in every minute way possible. I mean, why subject yourself to all the hassle and sweat of actually working for a living in a bid to become successful, when you can join the ranks of Jedwood on prime time television swearing, shouting, and completely embarrassing yourself in front of the Nations' eyes, in exchange for your fleeting chance of fame and fortune.

Turn the clock back, to a time not all that long ago when a person acquired celebrity status he or she did so purely because of their personal achievements, in their own chosen fields of endeavour: business, medicine, politics, science, designers, painters, writers, actors, musicians, directors and even gangsters! Men and women who had all reached the pinnacle of their careers thanks to their hard work, dedication, intelligence, determination and vision, who never gave up on their ambitions to be the best, no matter how many seemingly insurmountable obstacles life threw at them. Former 60's 'wild child' Jenny Fabian, took it one step further by saying. 'There was a time when all you had to be was cool' - and for thousands of people who grew up in the anarchistic revolutionary sex, drugs and rock and roll decade that changed the traditional dyed in the wool social tapestry of Great Britain forever, one man above and beyond description defined the word 'cool.' From the way he styled his hair, to the clothes he wore. He influenced the newly emerging 'youth culture' to the point, where every guy wanted to be him, and every girl wanted to be underneath him.

He was a dazzling one off metamorphosis of The Beatles and The Stones; all rolled into one. But what really set him apart from all the other mere mortals was his bottomless natural talent and ability to play 'the beautiful game', to a level only a select few footballers have come close to emulating. It was almost as if he'd been sent down from Heaven, as opposed to being born on Earth. Thousands of rival fans packed into stadiums across the country; instinctively coming alive as one, with a sense of excitement and expectancy from the second he walked on to the hallowed turf, to the final whistle blowing, for what they were about to witness.

No matter what he did both on and off the ball his presence and charisma guaranteed that every eye in the ground was focused on him alone as if the remaining twenty one players on the field were irrelevant; and they often were, after receiving a dose of his awesome talent and ability. He could be just standing there scratching his sideburns or hands on hips; figuring out his next move. He could be on the move: darting into impossible positions, deep in the opposition half, waiting to pass or receive the ball.

Then there were the moments when he really came into his own. Taking total control of a game about to be lost and turning it around into a draw, or a victory, within a few magical seconds. There would be a clear look of urgency beaming from his eyes, his posture exuding a realisation that it was 'time to go to work and earn his wages.' Countless times he'd pick up the ball, deep in his own half, signalling the beginning of another unique attack on the enemy's goal. The ball stuck to either foot like super glue, and he'd be off down the centre of the pitch; or on either wing with his own frustrated team members screaming for a simple pass to score an easy goal. But 'easy' wasn't in his vocabulary.

Seasoned hard defenders he simply ridiculed and humiliated hypnotising them into doing exactly what he wanted them to do. Poking the ball through their legs, or them ending up on their backsides, and he was gone. With only the panic stricken goalie to beat - dithering about on his line left, right, left, right, and left again. Diving the opposite way his shot was going, as the ball thudded into the back of the net, ending another lesson on how to score the perfect goal. A goal applauded by both sets of fans in recognition of his unique talent. Leaving him soaking up the moment in typical, simple understated fashion, one hand raised in the air, and a broad smile, with the odd handshake, or a pat on the shoulder from team-mates before the re-start - simple post goal celebrations devoid of all the embarrassing amateur theatricals modern day footballers' love to indulge in. No ten-metre long arms outstretched aeroplane glides over the turf, no tangled up group hugs; gripping and kissing one another like a bunch of love starved gays. No ridiculous robotic dancing, or group disco routine that would make Michael Jackson turn in his grave!

From the way he looked, and the way he played 'the beautiful game', he single-handedly changed the face of football. Shirt out of shorts, socks rolled down to his ankles. He set a new fashion far removed from the traditional Roy of the Rovers, stiff, short back and sides 'I say Sir, play up and play the game' image most footballers sported. Arguably 'The peoples' player' he possessed a bewildering arsenal of skills and ability that somehow transcended deep bitter rivalries for the sheer love of 'the beautiful game', and the way he played it so effortlessly. In every sense of the phrase, he really was 'simply the best' and then some.

ONE

Compared to the luxurious facilities today's ultra-modern football stadiums offer; players, managers, medical staff, spectators and officials, grounds in the 60's and 70's were primitive to say the least. Most had been built in the 30's, and they looked it, with many grounds needing serious tender loving care. Football clubs could ill afford offering creature comforts and health and safety regulations that are a feature of today's 'beautiful game.' Those of us who have reached a certain age, who can remember what football was all about back then, standing on terraces, freezing our nuts off frequently soaked to the bone, the game almost lost with ten to fifteen minutes remaining, but still we refused to call it a day for fear of missing some magical, match winning moment. All, part and parcel of the aches and pains that came as a result of being a football fan back in the 'bad old days.' From then to now football has evolved into two entirely different beasts, making it extremely difficult to explain to a modern football fan what it was really like back then, but a good way of going about the task would be to imagine you've just bought yourself a copy of the video game Match Day in the 60's and 70's, from your local HMV store. A well researched, multi-dimensional, audio-visual, realistic insight into a game nothing like the one played today. Crack open a few cold Buds, take your shoes off, crash out in your favourite chair, switch on the game and get into it.

The menu bar offers you many choices: where to start, and how to go about it. But in my humble opinion the best option is to start at the beginning, to give you the ultimate experience. So click on MATCH BUILD UP to get you in the mood after another long, hard, boring week's work, looking forward to the weekends 'fun and games' to begin. Click on the mouse and seconds later there you are walking into your favourite pub with all your mates, looking forward to a good pre match booze up, and a bit of aggro if it comes your way, as it frequently did from time to time. The first thing you'll notice are the football fans themselves older, down to earth, hard drinking, hard smoking, working class blokes, many of whom fought in the war. They are still wearing their work clothes after finishing off a Saturday morning shift, so they can have a few spare quid in their pockets. Flat caps, donkey jackets, overalls and boiler suits and not an Armani, Ralph Lauren or Lacoste label in sight; smoking full strength Woodbines and John Players like they're 'going out of fashion' and 'fuck catching cancer!' For these blokes, life is for the living. So why not have a good time while you can? Not a wealthy middle class chap in sight and no women and no kids to spoil the fun.

Back then football was a strictly male dominated, all shouting all swearing domain encompassing ninety minutes of freedom from the bills, the missus; going on about wanting a new colour television, and how useless they've turned out to be and how they should have listened to their friend's advice, about 'Marrying a bloke with a good secure future.' Half past two, quarter to three, and the mood in the pub changes noticeably as you feel the pre match vibe building up nicely. Kicking in with the beer and the couple of bombers you dropped in the bogs half an hour ago. The old boys' give you a stern look of disapproval, but keep your mouth shut, or you'll end up at the dentist with the man in charge about to rebuild your shattered mouth asking, 'How the hell did you managed to lose so many teeth?'

Football was simple back then, something to live for during the week. It kicked off at three o'clock and finished at quarter to five.

Time to drink up and march down to the ground; old blokes and young guns stand shoulder to shoulder, with ranks of coppers in Ford Escort panda cars and mark one Transit vans waiting for the aggro to kick off. Short, sharp, sweet, skirmishes with the away fans providing a taste of what was to come once inside the ground, picking them off one by one after the game en-route to the train station; until the next time, and there was always a next time!

Now you're enjoying the build up buzz. You'll find yourself outside the ground joining a long, impatient queue of fans waiting to get in via the turnstiles. Coppers bracing themselves as abuse and V-signs fly between you and the away fans, some fifty yards away. The queue getting smaller, until you're the next in line, at last! Turnstiles were a curious experience. Small confined spaces, secure and fool-proof with some faceless bloke sitting in a small box the size of a holding cell on death row, in the hours before the condemned man is led into the death chamber and the needle inserted in his arm, after enjoying his final meal: Strawberry milk shake, half a dozen Big Macs with large fries, the last thing he tastes as the warden gives the nod for the execution to begin. Pay your entrance fee, a few shillings or a couple of quid. Ridiculously cheap in comparison to what clubs charge their loyal fans today. Back then, you could watch ten games for what one would cost you these days! Soon as the man in the box counts your cash, he presses a button releasing the small cage like mechanism and you're in the ground, waiting for the rest of your mates to join you.

Wondering what to do next? Click the mouse on INSIDE THE GROUND and you'll be unpleasantly surprised at what you're seeing, perhaps even horrified at the facilities on offer; which are basically toilets and a fast food caravan. Best to take a leak now before you take your place on the vast, wide open, concrete, or timber terraces, packed with thousands of fans all glued to the game. No place there for a sharp exit to take a leak and grab a bite to eat. The stench of the toilet is enough to turn your stomach. Queuing up with other blokes with no privacy whatsoever, one in, one out, take a deep breath, steady yourself, and take aim at the open drain. As the urine of hundreds of blokes' makes you want to throw up and squeeze one out as fast as you can, before running out to the fresh air. Take a few breaths and get your head together. Maybe grab something to eat. But there isn't that much variety on offer, no Indian, Chinese or Italian cuisine served up in your exclusive rented private box 'For you my son!' No smoked salmon and cream cheese washed down with a chilled bottle of Moet Et Chandon suspended high above the pitch, as you snort 'Charlie' off the back of your thousand pound an hour nubile call girl. All you had back then was an old converted caravan knocking out urns of tea and coffee, fizzy-pop, Bovril and various pies, crisps and chocolates with plastic cups full of beer. You try your best not to spill a drop as you walk up the steps onto the home end terrace all the while as the nervous looking thin blue line gets ready for the aggro to kick off; trying their best to keep the battling fans apart.

The managers and physiotherapists take their place in primitive concrete dug outs with corrugated tin roofs sitting there like soldiers, waiting to go over the top, as the crowd hurled their vitriolic abuse at managers and players alike. The teams on the pitch minutes before the kick off, warming up, stretching, passing the ball about before the referee calls time and the ball is placed on the centre spot. The teams take their places, as the coin is flipped into the air - heads your team kick off, tails they don't - as you settle down to watch another episode of 'the beautiful game.'

This was the arena George Best stepped into way back in 1963, making the ball do exactly what he wanted it to. Effortlessly, skilfully, ballet dancer style, and tough with it when needed, which was often, with the ability to float over, or go through everything an opponent threw at him and then some; a crimson shirted, longhaired, Ninja imbued with unbelievable superpowers that everybody in the ground loved to watch. Love him, or hate him! He had them all under his spell, a young good-looking lad from Belfast, at the very top of, 'the beautiful game.'

TWO

In my opinion there have been six United number sevens who have possessed an array of extraordinary playing abilities which have contributed to them becoming world class players able to stamp their own individual authority on the flow of play, and turn a game lost into a game won, at the blink of an eye. All players who between them have collected every FA and FIFA honour and award going, over the years; the incredible atmosphere permeating through a packed Old Trafford crowd, especially on the big games, when losing wasn't an option. They demanded that the player wearing the number seven was a true artist and a showman, as well as possessing a sense of theatre and drama that allowed them to play their beautiful game with a confidence, and often arrogance, that true world class players are born with.

'Maturity brings many things. When I went to see them play against Manchester City, some of his decision making in terms of passing was brilliant; one touch passing, good crosses. In the six years we had him, you just saw his game grow all the time and he was a fantastic player. Now you see the complete player. His decision making, his maturity, his experience, plus all the great skills he's got make him the complete player.'

Sir Alex Ferguson's tribute to Christian Ronaldo - the first ever Portuguese player to grace the Old Trafford pitch, signed for a fee of almost twelve and a quarter million pounds during the 2002/ 2003 season. From the beginning of his United career, Ronaldo made it crystal clear to Fergie that he wanted to continue wearing the number twenty-eight shirt that he'd worn at his previous club. Fergie being Fergie, denied his request and gave him the number seven shirt instead, because of his extraordinary talent. Ronaldo accepted the decision as an honour, which motivated him to do his utmost to live up to the illustrious list of names that had gone before him, and he didn't disappoint; settling into his new role with ease, quickly establishing himself as a firm favourite with his new team members and fans alike.

During his time with United, what Ronaldo couldn't do with a ball wasn't worth doing. Able to play on either wing and centre field, doubling up as a winger and striker with the ability to wander around the pitch at will, switching positions as and when needed. On the ball he was defenders nightmare, with his lightning pace, dribbling, heading and shooting abilities from all angles. From the penalty spot he rarely missed such a free gift, making goalkeepers look like fools sending them the wrong way, as they clambered to regain their balance watching the ball slam into the back of the net.

Who can ever forget the sense of theatre and drama he naturally created with every trademark Ronaldo free kick? Slowly, carefully, stopping the play as he placed the ball down on the spot, like a golfer balancing his ball on a tee. The whole ground in silence, wondering what he was going to do next? As he methodically paced backwards to the required distance he felt he needed to give him a good run up to the ball. More theatre and drama followed as he stood legs apart, hands on hips, looking round the ground, eager not to disappoint the fans knowing exactly what he was going to do with the ball, to either make the moment his by scoring another sensational dead ball goal, or give one of his team mates the glory by delivering a pinpoint pass, so they could do the honours.

At the height of his popularity and talent Ronaldo started to believe all the hype that he seemed to be well on the way to becoming the world's greatest footballer. This, backed up by countless rumours that he'd had secret talks with Real Madrid with a view to leaving United, disgusted many United fans. He had blotted his perfect copybook by thinking that he was 'bigger' than the club who'd transformed him from a talented youngster, into a world class player. Despite countless attempts by Fergie to try and speak to him to fathom out the situation, Ronaldo continued to ignore all Fergie's calls - which is what you don't do when you're a Manchester United player, no matter how big a star you think you are - and player and club parted company in June 2009, granting Ronaldo his wish by signing for Real Madrid for a hefty eighty million pounds! Paying his eternal respects and thanks to Fergie, Ronaldo admitted that 'He's been one of the most important and influential factors in my career.'

David Beckham was born in Leytonstone, on the 2nd of May, 1975. A London boy through and through, who played football for his school Chase Lane Primary which was where he first displayed the kind of talent that would eventually transform him into not only one of the greatest footballers in the world, but also the biggest sought after advertising brand name. Had it not been for his parent's fanatical love of Manchester United, he would have definitely ended up playing for one of the top London clubs. But instead he chose United after signing a contract at the age of fourteen.

Following a promising appearance in the League Cup against Brighton and Hove Albion in 1992, he went on to sign his first professional contract that set him on the road to massive global fame and fortune. Becks soon became an integral part of the young United team nicknamed 'Fergie's Fledglings', playing alongside older, more experienced players like Paul Ince and Mark Hughes. After the latter's departure from Old Trafford, Becks inherited his number ten shirt with the number seven occupied at the time by the one and only Eric Cantona! Shortly after, the fiery Frenchman announced his retirement from football and the shirt was given to Becks to continue the spectacularly good work 'King Eric' had put in during his time at Old Trafford. A tough act to follow, but Becks shouldered the responsibility above and beyond all expectations; both for United and England.

He could read a game of football like a well-worn novel and this ability could change the course of a game, such as he did one afternoon against Wimbledon with a fleeting yet unforgettable moment of sheer impudent brilliance. Noticing the Wimbledon goalkeeper way out of position and giving him a chance to score the kind of goal all players dream of, sensing the moment was his and his alone Becks looked up and took his shot. A high ball arching through the air momentarily freezing the action on the pitch, before the ball floated, fully sixty yards, over the stranded goalkeeper and into the back of the Wimbledon net; giving United a 3-0 lead and the rest is history.

Becks also possessed an extraordinary determination and motivation that drove him on until the final whistle blew, an infectious energy rubbing off on the other players around him, running around like a human dynamo, such as during the 5-1 thrashing of Germany. And who can forget the moment when 'The Three Lions' were flagging during the qualifier against Greece? Destined for the exit until 'that' Free-kick, embodying a 'never say die spirit' the England team so badly lacked when it came down to the big Euro Championships and World Cup games.

Not to mention the unforgettable magic summer night in 1999, in the Nou Camp. Bayern Munich enjoying an early 1-0 lead over United as the game entering the closing minutes as they try everything to break through the staunch Bayern defence without success. With the FIFA officials standing by to engrave Bayern Munich's name on the cup, what happened next in the dying minutes of the game epitomizes the magic, the emotion, and the sheer unpredictability of 'the beautiful game.' It begins with a pinpoint Becks corner into the beleaguered Bayern penalty area; Ryan Giggs quickly passing the ball to Teddy Sherringham, who instantly slides the ball into the net; the 90th minute, one apiece, and everything to play for! Then another perfectly flighted Becks corner sails into the Bayern area finding Sherringham, who heads the ball downwards to Ollie Gunnar Solksjaer, lurking around in typical fashion, waiting to jump on the slightest chance of an equaliser, who stabs the ball into the back of the net. It's the 92nd minute, and Bayern are completely and utterly paralysed, as Manchester United go on, mere seconds later, to hoist the Champions League Cup for the second time in their history.

Enforcing the strict United philosophy that 'no one player will ever be bigger than the club', the rise of Becks as the biggest advertising brand in the world started to cause a rift between manager and player, with his wife Victoria by his side, backing his every move. Becks became the world's highest paid footballer thanks to various lucrative advertising deals that helped to distance him even more from football and Fergie, who had finally had enough, and in the summer of 2003 Becks was sold to Real Madrid for 35 million; a sad finale to a brilliant ten-year career with United.

Fergie once voiced an opinion that many United fans to this day still agree with. 'He was never a problem until he got married. He used to go into work with the academy coaches at night times. He was a fantastic young lad. Getting married into that entertainment scene was a difficult thing. From that moment in time his life was never going to be the same. He is such a big celebrity football is only a small part.' Many die-hard Reds' feel that under different circumstances Becks would have been with Manchester United for life; from the end of his playing career, to coaching, and eventually managing the club, but due to the crushing unforeseen pressures that go hand in hand with becoming the biggest global celebrity of his time, he had no other choice but to leave United. But what he did for Manchester United and England, the drama and excitement he tirelessly, unselfishly, gave us all, coupled with the unforgettable memories he left. We should all stand up and applaud David Beckham and wish him all the happiness in the world.

The 26th of November 1992, remains the blackest day for all fanatical Leeds fans in the history of their club. After a short career with them playing a big part in the 'White shite' winning the league, Fergie signed up Eric Cantona for a mere 1.2 million! Regarded as the steal of the century for the fiery Frenchman, who was affectionately nicknamed 'King Eric' by United fan faithful throughout his playing career. As was the case with Becks when he arrived at Old Trafford, Cantona was given the number ten shirt to wear, and he quickly fitted in well with his new team-mates. Equally at home storming down the wing, or taking control of the midfield. It was largely due to his contribution that United won the 1992-1993 season; United's first title since way back in 1967 and the first ever team to win the brand new Premier League Championship by a crushing ten points clear, making Cantona the first ever player to win two consecutive championships, with two different clubs.

From the get go, Cantona proved he was bristling with the ability and talent to make him a true United legend, prompting Fergie to award him the number seven shirt which he retained for the rest of his playing career. But just as he seemed to be riding high during the 1994-1995 season; trouble and controversy blighted his glittering rise to fame and fortune after he was sent off for a foul during the Crystal Palace game. As he left the pitch he was suddenly attacked by a gobby Palace fan telling him to 'Fuck off back to France, you French motherfucker!' An insult he assumed was aimed solely at his mother; hence the reason for his violent response. The FA was outraged by his behaviour and banned him from playing in England and Europe for eight months. He was given a joint fine of thirty thousand pounds from United and the FA.

Cantona was so disgruntled with the English game that he requested a transfer. But Fergie turned him down fully determined to keep him as a United player, and so after talks with the boss Cantona returned to Old Trafford vowing to stay there for the rest of his career. 'King Eric' was back, where he belonged, doing what he did best in charge of his distinctive number seven shirt with the stiffened upturned collar. United fans were overjoyed and countless times they showered him with their never ending adoration, the chant of 'Oohh aahh Cantona, Oohh ahh Cantona' echoing around the ground with everyone bouncing up and down wearing rubber Cantona facemasks, as he stood there like a proud Gladiator hands on hips, chest stuck out, proudly soaking up the atmosphere.

He continued to steer United to more success winning the Premiership and FA Cup in 1996. Scoring the only goal in the final against the 'Red shite' firing in a terrific shot from outside the Liverpool area that flew into the back of the net. The following season he was awarded the captaincy after Steve Bruce's depature, and once again he rose to the challenge as the driving force behind them winning their fourth Premiership in five years. He was at the pinnacle of his success and popularity, unable to put a foot wrong; but then once more, he shocked the football world by suddenly announcing his retirement from the game at the age of just thirty years old, leaving everyone saddened and stunned by his decision, knowing that he was good enough to continue playing for another five or six seasons before taking up a probable coaching position within the United hierarchy.

Reflecting on his time at Manchester United he summed it up in typical Cantona style. 'When you quit football, it is not easy. Your life becomes difficult. I should know, because sometimes I feel I quit too young. I loved the game, but I no longer had the passion to go to bed early, not to go out with my friends, not to drink, and not to do a lot of other things, the things I like in life. I'm so proud of the fans still singing my name, but I fear tomorrow they will stop. I fear it, because I love it, and everything you love you fear you will lose.' And of the Crystal Palace incident 'It was a great healing and memory. I am happy for the fans to treasure it - but it was a mistake' admitted the man voted 'United's greatest ever player', by the Insidc United Magazine.

Virtually from the get go of the thirteen years he played for United, Bryan Robson claimed the number seven shirt as his own, only surrendering it to 'King Eric' in the autumn of his long and distinguished career both for club and country. Beginning in 1974 when he signed for West Bromwich Albion, Robson played for West Brom for a total of seven enjoyable years, cultivating a good, honest working relationship with his manager Ron Atkinson, before the latter signed for United in June 1981. In the same season, while Atkinson settled into the Old Trafford regime, Robson's impressive succession of midfield performances for West Brom earned him his first full England cap, going on to make ninety appearances for 'The Three Lions' between 1980 and 1991. During which time he captained the team sixty five times, scoring twenty-six goals.

On October 1st, 1981, Robson signed for Manchester United for the sum of 1.5 million pounds, which was a record fee paid for a footballer at the time. According to Robson he claimed the main reason for him signing to United 'Wasn't about money, but the chance for him to become a winner.' And he did just that with: two Premier League Championships, three FA Cups, one Football League Cup, three Charity Shields, one UEFA Cup Winners Cup and one UEFA Super Cup during his career.

Robson's unquestionable talent made him a formidable attacking winger and master of the midfield for United and England. Scoring and creating goals with his pinpoint accurate passing ability and 'never say die' in-built determination, paving the way for Becks and Cantona. He was a huge favourite with the United faithful, scoring over ninety goals in almost five hundred appearances for United. As a tribute to Robbo's talent in August 2011, he was voted 'the greatest ever United player' by an assortment of his former team-mates.

Born in Liverpool in 1955, Steve Coppell was a natural footballer with a difference. He was playing for Tranmere whilst studying for a University degree when he signed for Manchester United in 1974 for the sum of sixty thousand pounds. Taking up immediate tenancy of the number seven shirt, in a United team that was then in the second division. Thanks to his performances, they returned to the first division in the same season. Coppell ended the next season with just short of forty appearances and ten goals to his name, as well as making his England under twenty-three debut.

In the 1976 season United were strong favourites to win the FA Cup against Southampton. But due to Southampton's much more experienced older players' they managed to pull off a surprise victory, beating the young, nervous Tommy Docherty led United by a single goal. On the day Coppell managed to produce United's only chance during a lacklustre game by hammering a twenty-yard shot in the second minute. The following season saw United back at Wembley against a treble chasing Liverpool team, United beat them 2-1, giving Coppell his first winner's medal. Coppell was called up for full England international duty playing in the 1978 World Cup against Italy. A game 'The Three Lions' won, but a competition they were knocked out of shortly after due to them failing to qualify. The week after, Arsenal lifted the FA Cup beating United in a nail biting final 3-2. Coppell turned out for England at Wembley beating the enemy Scotland 3-1, before going on to enjoy his two most successful consecutive seasons; both at club and national level.

Looking like he was destined to become a great number seven for United at the peak of his playing career, tragedy struck whilst playing for England against Hungary in the 1982 World Cup. A vicious tackle completely smashed his knee. He underwent an emergency operation where the doctors managed to patch him up well enough for him to continue playing in the entire main group matches, but he was forced to have a further second operation. The impaired Coppell continued to play for United for another season, but missed their FA Cup victory beating Brighton and Hove Albion 4-0 in the replay. Sadly, the damage to his knee was irreversible, and he was forced to announce his retirement from football putting paid to his rise to fame and fortune in a ten-year career. He was only twenty-eight years old, but he still holds the record for his two hundred and seventy three consecutive appearances for United between 1977 and 1981, scoring seventy goals in the process. A fantastic achievement in his all too brief career which makes him one of the great United players' who wore the number seven shirt, the way it should be worn.

There is a sixth player who not only wore the number seven shirt, but also claimed it as his own, for all eternity. Thanks to his unbelievable natural charisma, talent and flair for 'the beautiful game', he set the benchmark for all future number sevens' to aim for. His name was George Best, and he single-handedly changed the face of football forever.

THREE

On that glorious, unforgettable summer night, back in the summer of 1999, when Manchester United beat Bayern Munich in the dying minutes of the game to become European Champions for the second time in just over thirty one years, I watched the game from my rooftop studio in Brighton where I'd been living for some six years. A couple of hours later my best mate, who was one of the lucky United fans' to be there to watch one of 'the beautiful game's' finest moments, telephoned me from Barcelona, sounding like the celebrations were in full swing. Apparently, as the game appeared to be slipping away from United the television cameras panned around the ground, focusing on the United fans whose mood was understandably glum, when somebody shouts out for everyone to 'Make a show' and 'Smile' for the cameras. At that moment my mate looked to the sky and prayed. His prayers were answered a few seconds later, as United scored the vital goal they needed to propel them on to winning the game in the dying seconds. Talking to my mate; partying in the bars in Barcelona made me realise I hadn't been home to Blackpool for almost six years, and I suddenly felt that it was high time for me to spend a few days in the company of the mates I'd known all my life, Indulging in some overdue emotional pizza, spending some long overdue time reminiscing about the 'good old days', and catching up on all the gossip with friends and family.

So after a long exhausting train journey; thanks to a mechanical failure at Birmingham, I finally arrived in Blackpool, hours later than expected. Just enough time to grab a bottle of Scotch from the off-licence and a tray of fish, chips and mushy peas, before jumping into a cab to drop me off at my mum's place (who had a fit at the sight of me walking into the lounge unannounced).

After a brief chat with her, I telephoned up a couple of mates letting them know I was back in town and got the low-down on where we were to meet up on Saturday for a session. A couple of hot toddies later to help send me on my way, and I hit the sack.

The following morning I was up at the crack of dawn. Bathed, shaved and looking casual with it. Looking forward to a decent fry up to prepare me for what turned out to be a monumental town centre pub crawl, before a party at one of my mate's homes the same night. As expected, the party turned into a wild 'all night session', and as I watched the sun rising the following morning, dead on my feet, with a cold can of Carling for the hair of the dog I knew I needed my bed. As I was sneaking out to leave, carefully stepping over the snoring bodies out for the count, quietly opening the door so as not to disturb them, Karen took me completely by surprise. Sitting there, chilling out in the front garden, enjoying a bottle of Brandy and a Marlboro.

Back in the 70's Karen was Blackpool's answer to Bo Derek. A stunning, sexy, beautifully proportioned perfect ten, who could have pulled any bloke she desired with a click of a finger. Some twenty five years later Karen still oozed a rare sexuality with all her curves in all the right places. Looking drop dead gorgeous in a skin tight, low cut striped dress, high heels, Ray-Bans and long blonde hair hanging in the still warm morning air.

Knowing what I know now, I would have done myself the favour of a lifetime, if I'd have just given her a hug for old time sake and walked away without accepting a swig of brandy which led to an emotional eight year roller coaster relationship. Talk about those best-laid plans of mice and men!

After chatting for a while I agreed to join her for a stroll. Linking arms we headed towards Stanley Park for a walk around the lake, before spending a couple of hours sipping Cappuccinos in the stylish confines of the park's wonderful Art Deco café. Before I knew it, it was Tuesday and I was checking out twenty odd missed calls on my Nokia. Having spent four unbelievable days in Karen's little house by the park, enjoying what old friends who fancy each other do, when they suddenly find themselves thrown together for some reason or another.

We had spent most of the time in the bedroom with several bottles of Frascati and Brandy in between baths and hurried snacks, watched over the whole time by a large, framed, colour photograph of a sun-tanned young Karen in a bathing, suit standing next to an equally sun-tanned George Best in his shorts; both of them holding a glass of champagne in their hand, standing close to what looked like a Spanish swimming pool as she explained to me the circumstances behind the photograph.

Karen was fortunate enough to have achieved her lifelong ambition of becoming an air stewardess, working on short haul charter flights to Spain. The way she coloured her stories, it sounded like she'd had the time of her life before eventually leaving her career behind to get married and raise a family. Sex and booze parties in the cockpit with the aircrew being commonplace back then en-route to Malaga. Hiring secluded villas for a few days, where they continued partying in exclusive bars and clubs in Marbella where many celebrities chose to hang out, including George Best, who was coming to the end of his playing career with Manchester United, although they didn't know it at the time.

Flying back to Manchester Airport suffering hangovers, looking for a few days rest before doing it all over again and again and again, this was the time when Karen was on the top of her game; in the prime of her life and loving every second of her jet set lifestyle, rubbing shoulders with famous tennis players, racing drivers, golfers, actors and footballers all on the hunt for sexy, witty, women to hang on their arm.

Karen showed me an old photo album containing snaps of many celebrities she'd met on her adventures in Spain, including many with George Best. He in turn looked like he was having the time of his life, and why wouldn't he be, being one of the most talented, sexiest, men on the planet at the time. There he was in the bedroom watching us performing, as I wondered if Karen had ever touched down in his bed and if so, what was he like as a lover compared to me - A question I thought I already knew the answer to, hence the reason I never brought up the subject for fear of hearing the truth. Karen never touched on the subject either. Only telling me that "Georgie was a fabulous guy, with the world at his feet, out to have some fun with whoever fancied the idea of sharing his company' dreamily lost in the moment, staring at the photograph with a smile as she often did from time to time.

On the day George died, I was working in the Lake District a couple of miles away from the picturesque village of Ullswater, for a wealthy local farmer who was concerned about the total lack of affordable housing in the area for young people. As a result, he put his money where his mouth is, and decided to do something about it. He was renovating two large dilapidated stone barns with a plan to eventually sell them at well below the average price. I was recommended to him as a competent, professional, all round builder with a love of restoring old stone buildings. After a relaxed business lunch in Bowness, we shook hands after agreeing mutually acceptable business terms. It was November 2005, and the notorious Lake District weather had already set in with a vengeance, making every passing minute of my working day cold, wet and thoroughly miserable. Snatching time working in between torrential downpours, forcing me to spend countless boring hours in the cabin, drinking gallons of tea desperate for a break in the clouds to enable me to get back to doing what I was getting paid for. My morale was low, but the farmer was a fair man who knew I was doing my utmost to keep the project pushing forward and insisted on paying me cash every Friday, which was a Godsend to me at the time.

Karen and I had been together for some seven years and were living in Lancaster close to the castle. But by the time the rent, bills, council tax and Karen's drinking costs were paid for, little remained for enjoying a few pints in town or a meal in a restaurant. We were going through some bad times due to her escalating drinking, which had been going on for some time. This drove me to seek my own solace in the bottle when I came home from work every night, just to try to find some equal ground in a bid to keep our relationship together.

As a result there were countless times I used to turn up on site after driving sixty odd miles, nursing a heavy hangover, knowing full well that if the cops pulled me over and breathalysed me I'd be banned from driving, which would have ended my world, but what the hell 'In for a penny, in for a pound.' Ignoring the consequences of my stupidity on the day in question, I arrived at work greeted by the usual downpour drumming a beat on the cabin roof without a break in sight. I went down to the village café for an early breakfast, looking forward to warming my hands on a nice hot brew. As I sat down at the table nearest the fire waiting for my breakfast to arrive, a radio announcement literally stopped me in my tracks; the news that George Best had died in London's Cromwell Hospital, at the age of fifty-nine from alcohol poisoning.

I was so shocked I asked the waitress 'If it was true?' And she passed me a newspaper, the headlines and picture confirming the worst. A world without George Best seemed impossible to comprehend. I felt like crying on the spot. Staring at the tragic photograph of what remained of arguably the 'world's greatest footballer' pictured lying in his hospital bed, just hours before passing away. It was a truly harrowing image to take in. I didn't even know he'd been so ill for some time due to me being surrounded by the cocoon of problems I was having with Karen. I'd stopped reading newspapers as I had no interest as to what was going on in the world; and for the same reason, I banned myself from television news programmes, so I didn't have a clue how close to death George was when he was admitted to hospital several weeks before. He had died as a result of what he'd done to himself for too many years.

Public opinion was mixed, and vehemently so. With many arguing that he had nobody else but himself to blame for the way he died, after all, he'd been given a rare second chance of a new life thanks to the liver transplant many other people had been waiting many painful years to get. How many times had he gone on record with earnest promises to quit the drinking forever, only to hit the bottle once again, letting down all those who had loved and supported him over the years; equally so, there were many other people myself included, who remembered him for who he was, and the magic he created on the pitch. The sheer fear and intimidation he instilled in those poor unfortunates facing him, clueless as to which way he was going to turn and how to stop him, and the excitement of the crowds, who were fortunate enough to watch him in the flesh.

Many viewed his demise as a terrible tragedy, that he was a helpless victim of the very real disease of 'alcoholism' that affects those people it gets control of. The same way it did with him. Even during his final desperate days struggling for life, he took it all on the chin, like he always did after receiving a particularly brutal tackle; all part and parcel of the game of life and football, as far as he was concerned. He always refused point blank to blame anything or anybody but himself for a life blighted by alcoholism. The pictures of him splashed all over the newspapers were truly tragic. Weeks just lying in bed waiting to die, as his body deteriorated beyond all recognition and function. A ghostly spectre of the man every bloke wanted to be and every woman wanted to be under. His frail, pockmarked stained, skeletal form barely kept alive by machines and tubes.

With nobody to blame but himself! The photographs were accompanied by a poignant four word caption he insisted they printed, as a stark warning to others not to go down the same path he trod, and with perhaps a feeling of regret, from somewhere deep down in his complex personality, that given the chance, maybe he would have done it all so differently. The caption read 'DO NOT DIE LIKE ME.'

Almost seven months to the day George passed away, at twenty past two in the morning, on the 24th of June, 2006, my girlfriend Karen died in ward two of the Royal Lancaster Infirmary. Cause of death cited: massive attack of pneumonia brought on by cirrhosis of the liver, caused by acute alcoholic poisoning. Painfully similar to the way George had died. She was barely recognisable to the sexy, vivacious, woman I'd fallen in love with on that glorious sunny afternoon back in 1999, swigging brandy together, strolling around Stanley Park like two lovesick teenagers. We were oblivious to the sadness, madness and badness waiting to destroy us, in a way we could never have imagined.

Sitting by her bedside during the last hours of her life was a truly horrendous experience, knowing that only one of us was going to walk out into the sunlight. Badly jaundiced, a colostomy bag permanently attached, bedfast, stomach bloated solid out of all proportions. Her eyes only just visible; set back in hollow sockets. The ominous grinding noise of the death rattle as she lay there breathing through the oxygen mask covered in tubes, fighting desperately to hang on to life. Ten days before she died, I wheeled her out into the courtyard for one of her trademark Marlboro Reds. She told me what the doctor in charge of her treatment had told her; 'That there was nothing more he could do for her, except to make her as comfortable as possible, and that it was only a matter of time.' To be precise, seven days time was all the doctor had given her, at best. I was in bits at the news, sitting there trying to keep a brave face while fighting back the tears about to flow, trying to convince her that the doctor was wrong, and that she was going to pull through. False, shallow words, that were nothing more than a thinly veiled transparency to cover up the real tragic truth of the situation we were both about to face.

Karen just sat there calm and collected as if she was resigned to her fate. With a look of relief on her exhausted pockmarked face. 'Don't be upset Pete, just be strong for me, yeah? I never ever thought I'd end up like this, looking like this. I mean just take a look at me, like I did the other day in the mirror. I can't even recognise myself and to be honest, I haven't done for years. I'm so fucking worn out and unhappy living like this every day. I just want out of the whole thing. And I want to make sure you know that you had nothing to do with this, so don't you ever feel guilty.'

I'd asked her countless times when and why she started drinking, and all she replied was 'I can't remember a time when I didn't have a drink in my hand Pete. I was what, maybe thirteen or fourteen, I don't know? But the reason I like to drink is it gets me high, and when I'm high, I'm happy, and when I'm happy it helps me forget everything that's happened to me during my life. You know me well enough to know and understand what I mean Pete. Just promise me, you'll never forget me?' One of her final wishes that never materialised was that she told me she would have willingly allowed the final days of her death to be filmed and screened as a warning to others not to end up like her.

Five minutes before she died, a concerned nurse quickly checked her pulse telling me that she only had a few fleeting minutes remaining. As the nurse removed the tubes and the oxygen mask, she told me that if I wanted to hold her, then now was the time. The nurse left us alone, as I kissed her on the forehead, holding her close to me promising that I would never ever forget her, and all the crazy times we'd shared. But whether she heard me or not, is debatable? To this day, I've kept my promise to Karen; I'll never forget her, no matter what just like I'll never forget George Best and the terrible way alcohol destroyed two happy, smiling, sun-tanned people, who'd met each other in Spain some thirty years earlier, in an identical gruesome way who'd both given me so many unforgettable memories.

FOUR

With the date set for Saturday the 3rd of December, 2005, I'd already made my mind up that this was one funeral I was not going to miss. So, after work I hit the travel agents in Lancaster to check out the best options for getting to Belfast. I was planning on arriving a day or two before, to allow me time to find a hotel and have a look around the city. Sensing there was going to be some big business on offer, the airlines had bumped up their prices and at over three hundred quid return from Manchester to Belfast it was just too expensive. I needed some other options.

There were several night time ferries sailing from Liverpool to Larne and Belfast, with prices quoted around the thirty to forty quid return mark for a foot passenger which sounded okay. I had decided against taking the car over due to the massive traffic jams expected, coupled with the reality of driving around a city I was unfamiliar with. But the helpful girl behind the counter pulled a surprise 'rabbit out of the hat' informing me I had one more option available to me, which was an overnight berth complete with evening meal and breakfast for only sixty quid return, travelling on a container boat leaving Fleetwood at midnight bound for Larne. Now this I liked the sound of. It would also save me the hassle of having to spend time in Liverpool, as Fleetwood was only a few miles down the road from Blackpool.

Having lived in both Northern and Southern Ireland for some six years, I was already familiar with travelling on container boats, so as far as I was concerned it was a done deal. I handed the girl the cash in exchange for a return ticket. I was hoping for a relatively calm crossing, as opposed to the countless stomach churning crossings across the Irish Sea I'd experienced many times before. Endless boring hours spent holed up in the bar at Liverpool or Holyhead, waiting for the storm to subside enough, to allow the ferry to set sail. As expected, both the farmer I was working for, and Karen, 'hit the roof.' When I delivered the news that I was going to Belfast for a few days to attend George Best's funeral. 'What would you say if I told you that if you insist on going to Belfast, then you needn't bother coming back to work for me?' The farmer told me, both of us knowing full well that decent, well paid work was thin on the ground. There was a list of local lads ready to jump in my boots, to finish off the barns in time, but the farmer's ultimatum sailed over my head as I'd already decided that come what may, nothing and nobody was going to prevent me from paying my final respects to the 'Belfast Boy' who'd given me more excitement, enjoyment, and memories, than farmer Jim could ever do. Five hundred a week cash in hand or not.

'I'm telling you straight Jim. I really appreciate the work you've given me and as far as I'm concerned, I want to be the one who finishes off the barns for you because I like you, and respect you for what you're trying to do for the young people who live here. But no matter what, there's no fucking way I'm going to miss George Best's funeral. So you can either square me up what you owe me now and we'll part friends, or I'll see you in three or four days. You decide Jim?' What began as a goodbye confrontation, ended up as a thoroughly enjoyable pub meal in Bowness, washed down with a few pints of Theakstons and a couple of whiskies. The farmer under no illusion that no matter how much I needed the work to keep my sinking relationship barely afloat from week to week, I was going to Belfast and that was that. We both knew were we stood.

He stuck five hundred quid in my hand making me promise

him I'd be back on site at the earliest opportunity, after having had sufficient time to deal with whatever emotions I had to deal with, saying goodbye to one of the greatest footballers' the world has ever known. 'Thanks Jim. I can't tell you how much I appreciate your generosity, and I'll bell you as soon as I get back to let you know when I'll be back on site to pick up from where I left off. Weather permitting, eh mate?' We both shook hands and crawled back to our cars. Jim slowly pulled out of the car-park in his battered old series one Land-Rover, while I chilled out for a few minutes in my old Saab turbo. Turning on the heater and turning the stereo up full, listening to one of my favourite old soul classics 'You Don't Want Me No More' by Major Lance.

I sat there for a good half hour before a cautious drive to Sainsbury's in Lancaster, where I stocked up on enough supplies to keep Karen going for three or four days: bread, milk, pizzas, salad, eggs, vegetarian sausages, bacon and cottage pies, plus three bottles of brandy and vodka, half a dozen bottles of wine and a variety of soft drinks and mixers; before arriving back at one hundred and ninety one Willow Lane, and plucking up the courage to enter the breech once more, 'Or fill up the walls with our English dead.'

As usual Karen was on the couch wrecked. Watching EastEnders cocooned in a pink fluffy dressing gown, ashtray full of Marlboro Reds, and two empty bottles of brandy on the floor. Cracking open a third, as I walked into the lounge, weighed down with the shopping bags and the news that I was going to be away for three or four days; and that she had everything she needed to keep her going while I was away: food, booze, half a dozen packets of cigarettes, plus two hundred quid. As expected, she exploded on hearing the news that I was off to

Belfast. Howling and screaming to the heavens. Bombarding me with her usual broadside of insults that 'I was the worst man she'd ever known', 'I was crap in bed', 'I was responsible for her drinking', and that 'she hated me and wanted me out of her life, while she still had one.' Like water off a ducks back listening to her ranting, I dried myself off before packing enough clothes for my break. The abuse reaching a crescendo with Karen screaming at me to 'Never fucking come back. You fucking bastard!' As I slammed the door shut, dumped my bag in the boot and jumped in the Saab. Thankful for a few days away from the hateful madness our relationship had turned into. Slipping into first, and pulling away from Willow Lane infinitely happier than when I walked in half an hour earlier, looking forward to boarding the ferry that was going to take me far away from it all; even if only for a short time.

The first thing I noticed about the grey haired, middle aged bloke parking his midnight blue Bentley Arnage with a sumptuous off white leather interior next to my tired old Saab, was the record blasting out from his stereo; one of my all time Northern Soul favourites 'Stick By Me Baby' by the Salvadors. The second noticeable thing as he climbed out of his car smiling at me, was his sharp bespoke suit and overcoat. Single breasted, slim fit style, three piece semi-silver mohair number with a proper Crombie overcoat, polished Loakes black brogues and a silk Paisley scarf. Slamming shut the boot of his car he nodded and spoke to me immediately offering his hand in friendship.

'Hi there, the name's Robert, but most people call me Bob.'

'Hi to you too Bob; pleased to meet you, the names Pete. That's a nice suit by the way.' I replied shaking his hand firmly, as he spotted my shiny cherry reds nodding his approval. 'Thanks Pete, but it takes one to know one. You for Belfast or what?'

'Yeah, I've booked a cabin on the boat. What about you?'

'Same as you. I always use the cargo boats when I travel to Belfast, and if I don't see you before you grab a bite, I can highly recommend the chef's shepherd's pie. I'll see you later for a drink and a chat maybe?'

The cabin was small, but perfectly adequate for the needs of an overnight traveller. A mahogany panelled, ten-foot square space, comprising of a double bunk bed, a wardrobe; with enough room for two peoples clothes, a cramped shower room with a separate toilet and washbasin - all in all, a very cosy intimate interior. I dumped my bag on the floor, grabbed the bottle of whisky and climbed on to the top bed for a quick forty winks, aided and abetted by two large glasses of Scotch. I sat there, remembering the far happier times Karen and I had shared in similar cabins coming and going across the Irish Sea, and all our crazy adventures on the Emerald Isle. Times I knew were never coming back now. We'd gone way past the point of no return. But at least we'd shared some happy moments, and surely that had to be worth something, at some point in the future? Or at least I hoped it would. I woke up an hour or two later starving hungry, wondering where I was; the humming of the boats well-oiled ageing turbines, together with the noticeable surging forward motion telling me that we were ploughing our way through the Irish Sea on our way to Belfast. For what was not only going to be one of the most emotional days of my life, but for everybody else taking the time and trouble to turn out, to honour the memory of George Best for the final time.

After a quick shave and shower, I squeezed myself free of the tiny cubicle. Got dressed, splashing some after-shave on my face, before heading to the restaurant looking forward to trying Bob's shepherd's pie recommendation.

The restaurant was thinly populated despite it being big enough to seat between fifteen and twenty diners. It reminded me of a scaled down motorway service restaurant I'd spent countless hours in; travelling to and from Wigan Casino back in the 70's. Upon entering the room, several burly check shirted crew members looked me up and down, nodding to me, jabbering away in Polish or somewhere close by, as I checked out the containers full of piping hot food: curry and rice, macaroni cheese, spaghetti bolognese, lasagne and something bubbling away like a 'jungle swamp', that looked like meat and vegetable casserole; before being drawn by the savoury aroma of the shepherd's pie, which I ordered, accompanied by heaps of mushy peas, crunchy red cabbage and onion gravy along with a nice cold pint of Guinness to help wash it all down.

If anything the shepherd's pie tasted better than Bob described it, and I was already half way through it, seriously thinking of going up for a second portion when Bob appeared, giving me the nod for a second pint of Guinness. I sat there watching him laughing and joking with the chef, who loaded up his plate like he was a long lost friend before joining me on the chair opposite smiling as he raised his glass. Cheers Pete, all the best.'
'All the best to you too Bob!'
'How's the shepherd's pie by the way?'
'I've got to say, it's in my all time top three of all the ones I've eaten over the years. That's how good it is. How the hell does a chef working on a boat like this, manage to come up grub this good? He could give Gordon Ramsay a run for his money, no kidding.'
Bob laughed picking up his spoon, looking as if he was ready to steam in. 'He's been the chef on this boat ever since I've been using it, which is over nine years now. A right nice bloke, and a bloody hard worker with it. One night in here when it was his birthday, the skipper gave him the night off. So we celebrated

with a few bottles of malt whisky, and he finally agreed to give me his grandmother's shepherd's pie recipe. I've never eaten anything else on here since, well apart from the odd breakfast, and he does a mean fry up for those who can make it down on time after drinking a dozen too many the night before.'
'I'll remember that Bob, if I happen to surface on time.' I'm always partial to starting the day off with a decent fry up.

'But anyway, if you don't mind me asking, what brings you to Belfast?' I asked. Noticing the clothes he'd changed into after boarding the boat. An original stone coloured Baracuta Harrington, a nice old faded pair of Levi 501 red tabs, a check button down shirt and a pair of tan suede Clarke's desert boots. For a man several years older than me, Bob still looked 'cool as fuck!' A smart, sharp, understated down to earth bloke, who spoke with a warm down to earth northern accent. Who doubtless shared the same lifelong interests and influences as myself, making me as interested in finding out as much about him, as I knew he was about me. Two middle aged Mods, sharing identical similarities responsible for making us the men we are, and the way we've lived our lives.

'What brings me to Belfast? That's a good question Pete. But I've lived and worked there as a barrister since the early 70's, through most of 'the Troubles.' When Belfast was one of the most dangerous cities in the world to live in, and I don't mind admitting, that I've been close to death countless times over the years. There was one night whilst enjoying a few drinks in my favourite bar, when suddenly, the boys turn up and rake the place with a semi-automatic machine gun killing quite a few people, before they sped off on their motorbikes. And then the night I walked out of the Europa Hotel after a business meeting, seconds before a bomb went off in the foyer. The Europa was the most bombed hotel in the world, being blown up twenty eight times all told. Soon as the renovation work stopped, then BANG! They'd blow it up again, and more people would die as a result. But I'm still here to tell the tale, even though I wonder how the bloody hell I've made it though in one piece, when so many people many of whom were my friends and colleagues are lying six feet under in Milton cemetery.'

A sad appetiser to a story I never imagined I'd be listening too that night. As I agreed to Bob's suggestion that we swap the Guinness for a bottle of Johnny Powers whisky before he settled down to tell me more about himself and his life.

Leaving Lancaster Grammar School for Boys, with a clutch of O and A Levels' and good enough to get himself a place at Manchester University as an undergraduate law student with a passion for criminal law. Three and a half years later after graduating with a first class honours degree and an offer of a one years' pupillage with a chambers in the Inns of Court, Bob packed up his belongings in his Austin Healey, and raced down to the bright lights of London, dreaming of achieving his ambition of becoming a Criminal Advocate.

As a child he'd only spent a limited time in London. Family weekends away in the Alvis with his mum, dad and his elder sister Barbara. Countless enjoyable hours spent ambling around The Imperial, Natural History, Science and Victoria and Albert museums, Buckingham Palace and the changing of the guard. And the feeding times in the Regent Park Zoo reptile house, watching in horror as the keepers fed live cuddly bunnies, rooted to the spot terrified, as the giant Anacondas and Pythons slowly slithered their way over to devour their prey.
In between the constant pressures of studying a higher level

of law, Bob loved to hang around in Ronnie Scott's and The Bar Italia. Chatting up the girls in hip clubs like The Whisky A Go Go, The Flamingo, Ham Yard and Bag O Nails, gradually transforming himself from a fashion clueless teenager, to a cool, hip, Mod about town.

'And that's the way it's been with me ever since Pete. Those two years I spent in London, totally changed me, and it was the first time I had a clue about how to dress in proper clothes. What you see me dressed in tonight, is how I've dressed most of my life. Back then, I had my suits made up by a tailor in Peckham, who went under the name of 'Threadneedleman' because of his exceptional skill with the needle and cotton. The rest of my casual clothes I'd buy from shops in the West End, Carnaby Street, Brighton and what have you. London was the bollocks back then and during that time I lost my virginity, started taking speed and smoking dope and going to all the hip clubs and pubs 'burning the candle at both ends' until something had to give. And what gave were my legal studies. But I didn't fuck up altogether, I managed to pass my bar exam. I didn't do as well as expected, but nevertheless I managed to get a job with a criminal law practice for a year after leaving the Inns of Court, earning my living as an ambitious young lawyer by day, while I partied hard and fast all night, like it was going out of fashion.'

'Music wise, I've always been into jazz big time. That's why I liked going down to Ronnie Scott's whenever I had a spare hour or two. Unlike everyone I knew, who were into The Beatles, Stones and The Byrds. I just couldn't get into music like that, although I loved Georgie Fame and Dusty. I mean who doesn't love Dusty? Even now she can still bring a tear to my eye when I listen to her music. But what I was into in a big way back then Pete, were the R & B sounds they used to play in the clubs. I loved it Pete, Just so fresh and different. And after I saw Geno Washington live, well that was it for me; I was hooked on soul music for the rest of my life. As you yourself know the original mod scene only lasted for a short time.'

'A mate of mine, who lived in Manchester, invited me up for a long weekend. And I liked what I saw. The Twisted Wheel was putting on soul nights with the deejays playing the original sounds the London clubs had done before the scene broke up, and went into all that acid tripping, long hair, Paisley shirt scene. I stuck my notice in with the law practice when I got back to London, and moved up to Manchester.'

'A month or so later, I started working for a city law practice run by a barrister; who was a good friend of my Dad's where I worked until I decided to move to Belfast. Sorry Pete, for going on a bit, but I got a bit carried away looking at your Martens, they're a credit to you and it's been a long time since I've seen a pair that well looked after. But getting back to the question you asked me, what brings me to Belfast? I'm here for George Best's funeral. What about you Pete?'
'The same reason as you Bob. Just paying my respects to one of the greatest footballers I've ever seen.'
'Yes he was certainly that, and a lot more besides. He had the right name, the right image, and he arrived at exactly the right time when football needed him the most. I mean, he just wouldn't have had the same impact on the game if he'd have been called George Dawson or say George Smith would he?'
'Fair point Bob.' I replied. Emptying my glass, as Bob pointed over to Jan for another bottle of Johnny Powers.

FIVE

Having crossed the Irish Sea countless times in the six or seven years I'd lived and worked in Southern Ireland, I was all too familiar with just how cold and inhospitable it can be, especially during a winter crossing.

Ordinarily, I wouldn't have accepted Bob's invitation to share another bottle of Johnny Powers up on deck on the small seated area in the middle of the boat, but it was no ordinary night, and I was really enjoying the company, so what the hell. Two total like-minded strangers who'd met in a car park at midnight just a few short hours ago, sharing so much in common sailing to Belfast for the same reason.

'Yeah okay Bob. Sounds good! I'll go and get my coat and scarf and meet you up on the deck in five minutes.' I told him as he had a quiet word with Jan the chef, laughing as he handed a bottle of whisky to Bob with a 'No problem my friend, have a couple for me please?'

It felt like we were two brave adventurers embarking on an expedition from which there was no certainty of return. As I slammed the door shut and made my way to the enclave of timber slatted benches, where Bob had already set up base camp. We continued our pre-funeral wake with our collars up around our necks, reminiscing about the skill and beauty of a young George Best, at the top of his game, in full flight.

Looking back to that night, I'm convinced that if it hadn't have been for the amount of alcohol mixing with our blood, both of us would have been frozen to death come the morning. Two frozen, stylish, stalactites, clutching the remains of our whisky bottle; as Bob cracked it open, offering me the first swig, instantly warming me up from the inside out, sinking lower into my overcoat, as the chill of the Irish Sea cold night air nipped the back of my ears.

George Best was undoubtedly a footballer player who broke all the rules, both on and off the pitch. But the pitch was where he really did push all existing boundaries of how to play 'the beautiful game' to its extremities. Like no other who'd gone before him, and few since. A frail, tiny, tough as old boots, raggle-taggle gypsy; shirt out over his shorts, long hair flowing in the wind, casual, relaxed, but instinctively opportunistic ready to pounce on the slightest chance. Like a coiled Cobra waiting to strike!

Of course the awesome combination of these characteristics made him a magnet for getting fouled physically and verbally throughout every game he played. George took it all on the chin in typical fashion. Looking on the risks as being part and parcel of the way the game of football was played back in the 60's and 70's. Full of dirty tricks and moves that would have no place in today's modern game. Certain players' in rival teams anxiously waiting in the tunnel would shout and scream obscenities at him. Heated exchanges and solemn verbal threats that 'He was going to leave the pitch on a stretcher' and that they were 'Going all out to give him the worst time imaginable from the second the whistle blew.' And many were true to their word. Older, hardened, seasoned professional defenders' like Tommy Smith, Billy Bremner, Dave Mackay, Jim Baxter and Ron Harris. Iron hard, unfeeling, hit men, boasting reputations for stopping a talented attacking opponent any which way they could, often with their manager's full consent! Hatchet men, with the bare minimum of skills and ability, other than going full out to tear ligaments, smash cartilages, break ankles and legs.

Small wonder George Best's talent and style of play instilled fear, jealousy, inadequacy, and grim determination in those he faced, who had the often impossible job of stopping him with everything they had at their disposal, no matter what! Every team 'back in the day' boasted one or two ruthless hard men in their defence, and none more so than Leeds United of the late 60's and early 70's who had two of the hardest hit men going in Billy Bremner and Bobby Collins who had full approval from their manager Don Revie, 'To go out and do what they had to do at all costs to win the game.' Their style of grim 'do or die' football was the antithesis of the 'devil may care' attacking football Busby instilled and demanded from all his players', even if it meant United losing the game. They always went out and played it the only way they knew how. A tradition that is a strong feature of the current United team, often to the frustration and anger of the fans. Back then, the rivalry between United and the much hated 'White shite' was equally as fierce and intense as it was between United and the Anfield 'Red shite', with one noticeable difference. All the games George played in against the other league clubs, he never felt the need to wear shin pad protection, but playing against Leeds; they were essential kit to prevent him from being removed from the pitch in agony. With Revie's team sharing more in common with the game of rugby, than it did with 'the beautiful game.' Despite the ever present danger of a vicious tackle prematurely ending what was blossoming into a brilliant career, George took it all on the chin. With a famous joke he often repeated over many a drink or three in his favourite local when the subject of Leeds was mentioned. 'Why is the grass so green at Eland Road? Because they always put so much shit on it!'

Most United fans hated Leeds with a passion! And whenever we played them we always viewed the contest as the Yorkshire

White versus the Lancashire Red Rose, and we all knew who won that little argument. As I've always maintained, the best thing in Yorkshire, is the road out! Before the advent of televised football on the box, much of the early part of George Best's career went unnoticed; unless you happened to be one of the lucky people to be there watching him play live. But the press loved him. His simple, but appropriate last name, gave them plenty of regular opportunities to feature corny puns incorporated into feature headlines; and they really went to town. 'Best of the Best', 'The worst of the Best' and 'Booze, Best, behind bars.' All mirrored the ups and down's of his tempestuous career, both on and off the pitch, that to most of us who cared for him, took with the usual pinch of salt. Shortly after his first full league debut for United against West Brom back in 1963, even the most hardened cynical tabloid journalists knew they were watching a very special player. And the more they watched, the more they loved him. As his confidence grew allowing his skills to flourish and he started scoring goals on a regular basis. His name was almost a permanent feature in the newspapers. The more he made mincemeat of the seasoned hardmen who faced him, the more the press highlighted the defenders' lack of abilities to stop him.

Certain defenders' were asked for their comments on how they were going to handle the problem of stopping him the next time they played against him in the repeat fixture? Some responded making outlandish stupid comments that 'They were going to do to him either by hook or crook', building up an exciting prospect of a mini game within the big game, almost like some medieval jousting competition between the black and white knights of old. Side bets were placed on the outcome of the duel, while George remained silent throughout, confident that his skill and composure on the day would do all the talking necessary. Leaving a few of his adversaries making ridiculous claims that they would come to regret, and never live down throughout the rest of their careers.

One such man who was forced to 'eat his words', was the fearless, devoted, Chelsea hard man Ron 'Chopper' Harris, a man few attacking forwards' relished going up against due to his 'do or die' aggressive tackling style. The man who stated he was 'Going to nail George Best once and for all' in the oncoming fixture against United at Old Trafford. And so the duel was set, George Best versus Ron Harris like the gunfight at the O.K. Corral. In front of a packed, expectant, Old Trafford faithful, standing there soaked to the bone in the non-stop torrential rain turning the pitch into a soggy muddy morass, far from the perfect surface to enable George to get the better of Chopper Harris.

It was a misty atmosphere packed Old Trafford night in 1970, with visibility down to a minimum. As Johnny Aston kicked the ball high out of the United area, plopping down in the sticky mud. As Best appears, he picks up the ball going forward on to the Chelsea goal; with Harris watching his every move. Harris in turn waiting to make his move, in a bid to back up the words featured in the tabloids, as George pushes on. Harris sensing the moment is upon him 'do or die' or forever live it down, he slides in full bodyweight in a last gasp attempt to wrestle George off the ball. But George is already one step ahead, anticipating Harris's move with a minimal body swerve that's enough to send his opponent sliding into infinity and beyond, leaving second defenders' Hinton and Pete Bonetti at George's mercy. Knowing that every second counts before Harris gets back on his studs to run him down, George sells Bonetti a dummy and slams the ball into the back of the net. As Old

Trafford explodes! With George hanging onto the goalpost with one hand exhausted, his other hand raised in the air smiling away. Soaking up the thunderous applause for giving everyone another priceless moment in the career of George Best one - Chopper Harris nil!

Harris apart, George often admitted many times that out of all the teams he'd played against; and the grounds he played in, he really enjoyed the buzz of visiting Stamford Bridge to play Chelsea, a fixture that somehow always managed to bring out the best in him. In the seasons between 1963 and 1973, he played a total of eighteen league and cup games against Chelsea, scoring a total of four goals. Not a brilliant tally for a player of his immense skill and ability, but still four goals nonetheless, including a truly memorable one he scored on his first Stamford Bridge debut in September 1964, almost a year after making his first league appearance for United. And by all accounts what a debut it turned out to be! With the two rival teams' head to head at the top of the first division, the sixty odd thousand crowd packed into Stamford Bridge knew it was going to be one of those special games in which everything was to play for. But as it turned out, there was only one true winner that afternoon as United beat Chelsea 2-0; the goals courtesy of George Best and Denis Law who scored a memorable header from a perfectly placed pass from Best. That afternoon the 'Belfast Boy' tore Chelsea apart, making mugs of their seasoned experience defence. Accounts of the day state that 'He played a game of such mercurial skill and human dynamo proportions that even the Chelsea fans were fully appreciative of 'The peoples' player' and the way he controlled and commanded the game, from all angles the pitch had to offer.' Defence, midfield to attack, George played the game of his life. Weaving, bobbing and darting through his opponents with awesome ease, prompting the Chelsea fans almost to give George a standing ovation for his lesson in how to play 'the beautiful game', his way.

Half a century ago, and there he was with only one playing season under his belt firing on all cylinders, beginning his ascendancy to the top of his game. Playing the kind of football few people had witnessed before, but loved to watch. Just one year into his all too brief career with the promise of more magic to come, and what magic! Talking to Bob that night, the two of us all alone in the freezing cold dark night air, pushing through the waves to Belfast was a revelation for me. A good eight, or nine years older than me, hailing from a totally different background and profession from mine, and yet we'd walked down exactly the same adolescent path when we younger. Both of us into the same clothes, music and lifestyle; a carefree crazy time, living only for the weekends, mates, speed, music, booze and birds, neither of us denying the mutual love of the music we'd been into all our lives. Bob's original swinging 60's mod scene down in the clubs that played the early R & B sounds he used to dance to, being the same ones my mates and I danced to in Wigan Casino Soul Club back in the 70's.

Ordinarily when a bloke pulls up next to me on a car park in a Bentley Arnage, wearing the unmistakable cut of a Mark Owen made to measure whistle, jealousy would have got the better of me, prompting me to give the posh bastard a wide body swerve, purely because he appeared to have everything in life I could never afford. But when that posh bastard pulls alongside me in his Bentley with the sound of 'Stick By Me Baby' by The Salvadors blasting out from his stereo, well that's a different matter altogether. Not the usual commercial kind of music you hear blasting out from cars any day or night of the week. Which made me think, posh bastard or not, the man who shook my hand firmly after I complemented him on his excellent taste in music; had something about him, hidden depths that spoke volumes to me in the three days we spent together in Belfast.

'Nice sound you were playing earlier Bob mate. One of my all time favourite northern sounds, I haven't heard it in ages.'
'So you're into a bit of northern then?'
'Yeah you could say that. I went to Wigan back in the 70's, and had some of the best times of my life on the northern scene.'
'I know what you mean. I was lucky enough to spend some time in the Twisted Wheel in Manchester and before that, some of the clubs in London when the scene was just starting out. Mind you, the scenes changed a bit since then, don't you think?'
'You can say that again mate. There are new soul nights springing up all over the place, even in Europe and Australia. And the Jap's and the Germans are buying up as much of the original vinyl 45's they can get their hands on. The prices for them these days are outrageous. That's why a lot of the new deejays use CD's now.'
'That's a shame Pete lad, because you can't beat the sound of vinyl singles the cracks and the hisses before they start playing. That's why I spent a fortune to have a proper Technics record deck fitted in the boot of my Bentley, converted to play all my original singles. All I have to do is press a button, sit back, and I'm right back there on the dance floor at the Wheel.'
'Now I am seriously impressed Bob!' I exclaimed. Wondering what it would be like living life in such luxury, as he stood there laughing at me shaking his head.
'Have I fuck Pete lad. What do you think I am? Made of money?'

As the whisky really started to kick in, we started going down that twenty question road to nowhere: favourite book, film, food, era, holiday destination, music etc, when the impossible subject rose to the fore. Which was; what was the best goal George ever scored? A question that instantly brought to my mind that old storming Tamala Motown classic 'Needle in a Haystack', as I sat there trying to recall one special goal above all his others that stood out head and shoulders above the rest, but to be honest, I was stumped. That moment sifting through my alcohol addled brain, almost frozen in a state of cryonic suspension courtesy of the Irish Sea, I somehow managed to focus on one goal in particular. Out of all the ones he'd headed, dribbled, twisted, weaved and shot into the back of the net, leaving witnesses spellbound and begging for more.

Tottenham Hotspur visiting a packed, venomous Old Trafford with their golden boy, star forward Alan Chivers. Proudly sporting his new pair of bushy sideburns thinking he was the bollocks, and to many he was. During a Spurs attack he was brought down to the penalty area, earning a free kick on goal facing the one and only Sir Alex Stepney in goal; a formidable keeper to beat at the best of times. So loud and unnerving was the sound of the chanting bouncing all around the ground 'Chivers is a werewolf, Chivers is a werewolf' that the referee refused to allow the penalty to be taken until calm was restored. Then for a brief time it was, as Chivers steadied himself concentrating on slamming what was a 'gift horse in the mouth' past Stepney, into the back of the United net. The ref blew his whistle signalling for play to resume, and the noise started up again. Chants and whistles, scoreboard-enders waving their scarves, bouncing up and down flicking Chivers V-signs; the only deal he was going to get from the Old Trafford faithful. As if resigned to his fate, Chivers ran up and struck the ball over the bar, the whole ground erupts in a volcano of abuse and ridicule 'Chivers is a werewolf, Chivers is a werewolf.' Shaking his head, hands on hips realising he'd blown his big moment.

As play resumed it was time for George Best to step into the spotlight to play an unforgettable part in the game, which is cemented in Old Trafford folklore as deep as King Arthur's cherished Excalibur buried deep in the magic stone. A goal that began with United attacking the Spurs defence who quickly organised themselves into a wall ready to repel whatever United were about to throw at them. Completely oblivious to the genius George Best was about to unleash on them a second or two after the ref blew his whistle for play to resume. What immediately followed was a spontaneous, brilliantly executed, first touch of the ball; a simple lob high in the air catching Pat Jennings off his line momentarily, but far too late for him to stage any kind of respectable recovery. A mathematically, precise calculation, combining lift, velocity and gravity that dropped under the goal post, leaving Pat Jennings scrambling and crawling helplessly. The whole ground once again erupting in joyous celebration of another simple George Best moment, which was anything but simple! Proving yet again that he was an outstanding player, far ahead of his game that was often quoted as saying 'That once I'd made it into the first division, I knew it would be easy for me to play the kind of football I wanted to play.'

Normally I've never been jealous of older people; one step nearer the grave barring accidents and all that, but I was of Bob; because of the fact that he'd watched George Best in his early years. The years when he was ascending into the global superstar he was destined to become.

Bob was totally honest with me that night, up on the freezing cold deck, explaining that he was never a big football fan in the sense of the description, unlike his Dad who was a regular at every Old Trafford home game. Despite years of constant badgering from his Dad, who wanted nothing more than his son to be standing at his side watching the game, Bob wasn't interested one bit in 'the beautiful game', and besides, at the time when every spare moment counted, his sole ambition was to become an accomplished barrister with a long, secure and fruitful career ahead of him. Before the swinging 60's took precedent over everything he did. Before music, fashion, drugs, booze and birds became the reason for him spending so much time at an entirely different bar, to the one he'd anticipated!

It wasn't until Bob moved back to Manchester, in the mid 60's, that he finally acquiesced to his Dads pleas 'To come and watch United and their new player, a handsome young lad from Belfast called George Best' who was setting the pitch on fire with his uncanny skills and ability.
Ever since making his first team debut back in 1963, as well as playing a major contribution in United winning the 1964-1965 league championship after a tense nail biting battle with the 'White shite.' With George scoring one of the three goals in a home win against Arsenal. The mood in the team was one of hunger for more successes, with George's appetite bigger than most to win more British and European trophies. And he didn't have to wait too long to finally make his appearance on the stage his heroes: Puskas, Garrincha and Pele had made their second home. Both the European and World Cup competitions George longed to play in, to enable him to show the world the kind of dynamic player he was, and the skills he had at his disposal.
'I can't tell you how many times my old man hassled me to go and watch a game with him at Old Trafford, even though he knew I had no time for football, and never did have. But he kept going on about this special United right winger called George Best, and that I had to see him play, if only once, while I still had the chance. Before one of the major Spanish or Italian clubs came in with an offer he couldn't refuse. I must admit, I was more than a little intrigued after listening to all the hype my

old man told me about him, and the way he took the game of football to a whole new previously unmatched level.'

Everyone who watched him play knew they were in the presence of unparalleled genius, and that people would be talking about George Best years after he'd hung up his boots, much to the relief of all defenders.
'Saturday afternoon, October 9th, 1965, was the very first time I went to Old Trafford to watch United play against the Anfield 'Red shite.' My old man was excited as hell. Me standing there with him, as we watched this long-haired, skinny, young boy, play a brilliant game of football, scoring a goal in a 2-0 home win against the 'Scousers.' From that moment on, I was well and truly hooked by football. Well no, I tell a lie, not football as such, but by the way George played it. Realising that everything my old man had told me about him didn't even come close to mere exaggeration. Or watching what he could do with a ball live, everybody in the ground, even the 'Scousers', got excited when he got the ball. Wondering what magical trick he had up his sleeve next. The whole ground jealous of him, because not only was he the most talented player we'd ever seen, but he was good looking with it, and there's nothing more annoying to a bloke than another bloke whose good looking and talented.'

'From then on I rarely missed a home game with, or without my old man at my side. Honestly Pete lad, I know I don't have to tell you of all people having watched United in the 70's, you saw it and heard it for yourself, but the atmosphere in the ground back in the 60's was unbelievable. Just like the memories you and I shared back on the Northern Soul scene. Every game I watched George in, he just seemed to get better and better. Having more tricks up his sleeve than a circus magician. But that was back in the day when teams played far more games than they do now.

Forty odd league games, plus all the games competing in: the FA Cup, League Cup, Charity Shield Cup, Inter City Fairs Cup and the European Cup, which was the one trophy every team wanted to win.'

'It was during the 1966 season, when I went to watch United play against Benfica in the Stadium of Light in Lisbon. The game regarded by many as the perfect opportunity for George to show the world what he had to offer the game of football. Despite Benfica beating United 3-2 at Old Trafford and gaining the all important advantage of an away win, and a probable victory against United. I was determined not to miss the away leg in Lisbon. We all knew it was going to be almost impossible to beat Benfica, who were a team on top of their game. Widely tipped to become the new European champions, especially in the Stadium of Light that was the graveyard for so many clubs, but the feeling between the United fans was that come what may, we were going to go to Lisbon and give Benfica a bloody good run for their money! And if they did turn out to be the winners, then we'd go down fighting in typical United fashion.'

'From the moment we hit the bars around the stadium, we were all in a good mood, having a friendly laugh and piss-take with the Portuguese fans. They were already giving us their sincere condolences for having wasted all our money coming to Lisbon to watch United get hammered, by Eusebio and his boys. Without either mob of fans realising just what was about to happen, especially the Benfica fans, who were all shocked and stunned. Legs rooted to the spot, as the final whistle blew. And United walked off the pitch 5-1 winners, after delivering the biggest humiliation and lesson on how to play 'the beautiful game' the mighty Benfica had suffered for ages.'

'And talking of great nights… I was in the Nou Camp back in the summer of 1999 when we beat Bayern Munich in the dying minutes of the game to win the Champions League. And what a feeling that was Pete, because it was the miracle we never truly expected to happen. Bayern thought they had it in the bag, and we were beat on our feet after throwing everything we had at them without any success. Those last few minutes were mental, as David Beckham sent in those two perfect made to measure corners, which in many ways was identical to the way George Best destroyed Benfica, but the opposite way round, if you know what I mean? That night in Portugal the crowd was over seventy thousand strong, and we were all expecting something magical to happen in order to win the game, the way the European Cup final should be won. And George sensing that it was his moment to hit the world headlines stepped up to the mark, in spectacular fashion, determined not to disappoint the expectant crowd and smashed Benfica to bits in around ten minutes or so. With none of us actually believing what we'd seen: a one-man demolition job on the Portuguese defence, scoring two unforgettable goals. I can still see it clearly now, after all these years. The first one he knocked in was a brilliant header, from an impossible angle of a high ball. Even the mighty Rio Ferdinand would have trouble getting near. For a small player George could head high balls for fun, and from all angles, with the balance of a ballet dancer.'

'We were all still catching our breath, when minutes later he scored a second goal in typical Best style. Latching on to a pass from I think it was David Herd, and off he goes like lightning charging down on the Benfica goal, looking like the defenders didn't have a sniff of getting the ball off him. We all knew he was going to score, but what a goal, Pete lad! Watching him dribbling through three or four players one at a time, leaving them for dust, making everything look so bloody easy, the way he always did.'

'That ten minutes well and truly put George Best on the world stage, like he could never have imagined. He became the first ever football superstar, and he knew it. His life was changed forever and the pictures of him getting off the plane the day after were hilarious, with him wearing a massive Sombrero which kind of suited him in a weird way. As all the tabloid headlines nicknamed him 'The fifth Beatle' and the rest is history.'

'The last time I went to Old Trafford to watch him play was in September 1970, when he scored a goal in a 2-0 home win against Everton. A year before 'the Troubles' in Belfast started to get ugly. I was more than a tad bored with my comfortable lifestyle prosecuting robbers and rapists day after day, and I felt like I needed a big change in my life to help give me a true sense of the advocate I wanted to be. And Belfast even though I'd never been to the place before, well it just seemed like the place to be, as far as I was concerned. '

'The Catholic population were having a terrible time of things, persecuted by the Protestant majority. In a strikingly similar way to how the Jews were treated in Germany before the war. Sectarian violence on the council estates was increasing every day. People were set upon, dragged from their cars and homes beaten helpless, and their property set on fire. The situation was a ticking time bomb waiting to explode, as the Catholics started fighting back. So thinking that they'd put a stop to the escalating violence, the labour government under Harold Wilson sent in the troops to protect the Catholics, without realising the damage they were doing by sending in the Argyll and Sutherland Highlanders on to the streets and council estates of Belfast.

They could not have got any more Protestant in their beliefs. Instead of them protecting the Catholics, they sided with their Protestant brothers and sisters doing the exact opposite job from the one they were sent in to stop; a short sighted, badly planned cock up, which gave birth to 'the Troubles' that plagued Northern Ireland for decades. And thousands of people: squaddies, civilians; young and old alike, all killed and maimed in the name of sectarianism. Why I'm telling you all this? Is to get the point across that George Best was born in 1946, and you know what? Thank God that he was born then, because if he'd have been born say a decade later, around the same time as you were born Pete, there's no doubting the chance of him going down the same road as hundreds of other young Irish lads by joining the IRA and fighting for the free Irish cause. It would have been impossible for him to have walked away. Think about it Pete. It would have been another pointless waste of a young life and the world would never have heard the name of George Best, or seen him play football. And how sad and tragic would that have been? Not that we'd have been aware of his existence. I mean, you know the old saying Pete, 'we never miss what we've never had' do we 'eh?'

Bob was spot on in all he was telling me, and chillingly so. I found him thoroughly fascinating to listen to. His stories of watching the young George Best sending out his early message to the footballing world, that he was a unique player bristling with natural talent and ability that was going to make him one of the greatest footballers in the history of the game, instead of ending up in a grave surrounded by grieving family after being shot or blown up by a bomb. And on that poignant thought, Bob took a swig of whisky before handing me the last mouthful. Smiling as he looked at me, with tired tearful eyes,

'To George Best! 'eh, Pete lad. Let's hope he gets the send off he truly deserves.'
'I'm with you on that one Bob. To George Best! For all the great memories and moments he gave all of us who love football.'
Emptying the last of the whisky down my throat, throwing the empty bottle out to sea we both hauled ourselves to our feet, bones frozen stiff. But it had been worth it. As we shook hands, looking forward to getting our heads down for a few hours sleep in a warm, cosy cabin, before docking in Larne and setting out on the most poignant part of our pilgrimage.

SIX

I was clueless as to the time when I finally scrambled into my bunk bed, fully clothed, sinking into an instant deep coma seconds after switching off the light. But the following morning, staring through the porthole, blurry eyed at the Irish Sea getting my bearings, I felt uncharacteristically 'top of the morning', considering the amount of whisky we'd shifted. Glancing at my watch it was half six. I had a full day ahead of me. Meaning that in another hour or so, we'd be arriving in Larne, where I'd have to jump into a cab to take me to the train station for the twenty or so minute journey into Belfast city centre. Wondering what my next move would be? Pick a hotel or bed and breakfast at choice. Or quiz the cabby. Asking if he knew a reasonably priced place where I could lay my hat for two or three days. A comfortable room, where I could chill out for a few hours submerged in a warm, soapy, neck deep bath, with a couple of whiskies before checking out a few bars. Asking questions as to where and what time George Best's funeral was taking place? And the best vantage point to wish him all the best, as he drove by?

After three barely palatable cups of slushy, hot watered down coffee granules, sugar laced with generous measures of whisky listening to Weller's 'Changing Man'; wondering where and when the change I badly needed was going to take effect. I started to feel like I was firing on all six cylinders.

After a quick shower and shave, scraping away the sticky fur lining of my teeth and mouth, I dressed casual courtesy of a pair of white Levi's, suede Clarke's tan desert boots, a horizontal blue and white striped wool crew neck jumper and a stone coloured Harrington. I sat, stretched out on the bed, enjoying the gentle swell of the boat with a large hot toddy, looking forward to one of Jan's breakfasts. Determined to start the day off how I needed it to go on.

Bob had beaten me to it. Looking 'bright eyed and bushy tailed' sitting at the table we'd shared the night before, telling me he'd been rather presumptuous in ordering me breakfast. I joined him, sitting opposite. As I filled up a mug with steaming hot coffee and cream, as the sight of a large pot bellied man with a shaved head and handlebar moustache, similar in age to Bob, wearing a red Cantona Manchester United shirt walked into the kitchen. He was piling up food on his plate as he walked down to the end of the counter, looking around the room for some early morning conversation, as he paid his bill, whilst we sat there trying to avoid him.

'Good night last night Bob, I really enjoyed talking to you even though I don't have a clue what time it was when we hit the sack? I can't believe I'm feeling hungry after the amount we put away last night.'

'Yeah I've got to admit, I was feeling as rough as a bears arse when I got to my cabin. But I'm feeling surprisingly okay today Pete.'

The perfect cue for our big friendly chef to appear handing us two of the biggest breakfasts imaginable, with a big welcoming grin and a 'Please gentlemen, I hope you enjoy my breakfasts, yes?'

Bob was spot on as usual as he described the food as a 'Cholesterol mountain' and what a climb it took to get to the summit. Watching Bob empty the contents of an antique, engraved, silver hip flask into both our coffees. No questions asked, or necessary. The familiar whiff of whisky wafting under my nose, as Belfast slowly appeared in the distance through the rain and mist.

The crossing had been unusually calm and effortless, compared to the countless times I'd done it with Karen. Sitting for hours rolling around on the top bunk unable to sleep as the boat pounded through the waves, while Karen filled up the cabin with cigarette smoke, continually drinking vodka or brandy before passing out in a coma; more often than not just before we docked, as the tannoy announcement requested that 'All passengers with cars please make their way to their vehicles in the loading bay area.'

You cannot possibly imagine the aggro and embarrassment of waking Karen up from one of her drinking comas, trying to make her understand that we had to make a move. Getting her dressed, her case packed and steering her down the corridor and stairs in one piece. She in turn thinking it was all one big laugh. With me struggling to keep her from falling over, as she continually swigged brandy craftily disguised in a coca cola bottle, so as not to draw untoward attention to the fact that she was 'pissed out of her brains' at half six in the morning… again!
Cackling like a demented banshee, as I squash her into the passenger seat as discreetly as possible, with her shouting and swearing at me, until eventually things calmed down, as she ran out of venom and passed out on the fully reclined seat, snoring like a trooper. Small wonder that during the many crazy moments we'd spent travelling back and forth to Ireland up on deck, just the two of us all alone. Sipping our chosen poisons, each in our own world of pain and bitterness. Thinking to myself, that all I needed to do to get rid of her forever was to grab her by the collar and push her overboard, leaving the ice cold waters of the Irish Sea to do the rest; never to be seen again. And nobody would have been the wiser, apart from me of course.

All the while sitting there with Bob, watching him wiping his plate clean with his last slice of toast, I'm momentarily lost in the past, all the good, bad and ugly moments we'd shared in the eight years we'd been together, both the madness and the badness. The moments and opportunities now lost forever, and blaming myself for Karen's demise, when we were approached by the pot bellied man in the Cantona shirt.

He introduced himself to us as Otto. He was a German guy around the same age as Bob who worked for BMW. He shook our hands like he meant it before producing a bottle of vodka that he invited us to share with him before docking.
'Course you can join us Otto, sit yourself down there.' Bob said. Looking at me resigned to the fact that we were about to experience one of those, 'in for a penny, in for a pound' situations, there was no escaping from, as we listened to Otto giving us a brief history of his life. Where he was born, how he became a lifelong Manchester United fan and why he was travelling on the same boat to Belfast as we were.

Otto was a likeable giant of a bloke, and funny with it. With a chubby well lived in face, pinprick eyes and a shaved head. He was born in Leipzig, East Germany, shortly after the war ended. His mother worked as a schoolteacher. While his father was a career policeman who'd managed to dodge military service due to him being in protected occupation shortly after the Russians erected the monstrosity of the Berlin wall. Separating the East from West due to his extensive police career stretching over twenty five years' service.

His father Felix put his talents to good use by joining the STASI secret service, investigating all known anti-communist activists and dissidents. A decision he made purely and simply to support his family, rather than harbouring some blind devotion to comrade Stalin. Feeling that it would be far more fortuitous for his family, to work within the system, than outside it, his rapid rise through the ranks was meteoric, from a lowly uniformed copper pounding the beat night after night, to a plain clothes Commissar with his own office. A considerable private caseload and personal secretary weren't the only privileges Felix Rudel enjoyed. The job, or rather his position, came with a Volkswagen Karmann Ghia and the family fridge filled to the brim with the kind of food other families only dreamed of eating: fresh meat, fish and vegetables. No doubt, a most satisfying change to the tasteless greasy gruel they'd survived on for years. As well as total freedom of passage between East and West Berlin, as and when desired, operating under what he loosely called 'official party business' in reality nothing more to the Rudel family than enjoyable family shopping days in the land of democratic affluence, stocking up on as many luxuries as they could fit in their car, without warranting a vehicle search at Checkpoint Charlie, before a grudging return to the dreary poverty-stricken austerity of life in the Eastern Bloc.

'I really loved growing up in the 60's, when my father took our family to Berlin for days out' Otto began, as he poured out equal measures of vodka into our mugs and continued. 'Because of my father's power and influence, the communist border guards didn't have a clue as to the real reasons we used to go to Berlin, so many times before my father became a commissar.

I can't tell you how terrible life was for people on the other side of the Berlin wall. Clothes, food, work, money; everything was in such short supply. People did anything they could to make their lives happier. So many of my friends families living in poverty while we were doing well, and yes, I felt sorry for them. But it was 'dog eat dog' back then.'

'To everybody in the east the west seemed like a magical kingdom, like Camelot itself. And many died trying to escape the east. Terrible times like I say. If the border guards had suspected my father of bringing in what they called 'contraband', we'd have all been sent to a Siberian Gulag for sure. I used to spend what spare money I had buying up as many pairs of Levi jeans as possible, to sell to my friends for a small profit because everybody wanted American jeans and Wrigley's chewing gum back then. I couldn't get enough of the stuff, I tell you. Later on whilst living in Hamburg training to be a motor mechanic. There was what you used to call a very 'happening' music scene going on, in many of the clubs. In fact, I saw the Beatles play a number of times. They were fantastic! And they were a big influence on me, and all my friends. We grew our hair long like them, and we wore the clothes they wore; two piece slim suits and Winkle-picker boots. We all thought we were very hip and I started playing in a group.'

'For my birthday, God knows how! My father bought me a beautiful Rickenbacker bass guitar. We played pop music mixed in with some rock and roll and blues, we were called The Mental Criminals and we played quite a few gigs in the clubs in and around Hamburg. And we almost managed to get a recording contract, but my father he wouldn't allow me to put my music before finishing my apprenticeship, so I became a mechanic instead of a bass playing pop star. Part of his concern for my future, I could understand, and I've done well since I joined BMW fifteen years ago. But even so, I often think how things would have turned out for me if I'd have had the courage to follow my musical dreams.'

'Just one of the many enjoyable luxuries my father's position allowed him to acquire, was a television. Something nobody owned where we lived in Leipzig. Admittedly, it was small and primitive compared to today's sets. But back then it was magical to be able to watch programmes. My father's big passion was football, and he was a big fan of Manchester United. We watched the 1968 European Cup Final on the television, in a hotel room his friend owned. That was the first ever time I saw George Best play football. My father told me he was the 'greatest player in the world', even better than Pele was, and that was saying something! I was so looking forward to watching him that night; because he looked so different to all the other footballers' I'd ever seen, with his long Beatle haircut. Honestly, I could not take my eyes off him the whole game. All of my female friends wanted to fuck his brains out, and all my male friends were so jealous of him because of this. But who could blame them? If I had been a woman, I would have loved to fuck him to. I watched him play quite a few times after the European Cup Final, and he seemed to play a lot better than he did that night in Wembley. Although he scored a fantastic goal, he didn't play as well as he could. But you can't play your best every game. He gave me so many memories, and I couldn't believe it when he left Manchester so suddenly at such a young age, just the same way Eric Cantona did. It's a great shame when such great players leave the game too early, because they deny us the enjoyment and the privilege of watching them. This is the reason why I felt I had to go to George Best's funeral tomorrow, to thank him for all the memories he gave me. If you're a true fan, and love football, tomorrow is going to be one of the saddest days in the history of the game.'

Even now, when I remember that morning, I look on it as one of the most enjoyable experiences I've ever had. There we were, three strangers drawn together for the same reason. To pay our respects to a man who'd given each of us so many different, yet identical magical moments thanks to his immeasurable skill, talent and charisma. It was around seven in the morning when we finally docked in Larne, some half-hour behind schedule. But so what, schedules were out of the window on that cold grey morning. The three of us sitting there, half pissed, facing a long emotional two days as we split what remained of the vodka in a final toast to George Best, as we slipped into Larne after a surprisingly enjoyable journey. Before preparing to disembark, the three of us stood up, shaking hands. Wishing each other all the best of luck as well as promising to try and bump into one another at some point in the next two days; knowing full well that was never going to happen, due to the amount of people invading the city to say goodbye to their 'Belfast boy.' But sentiment comes free, and the thoughts and wishes we expressed were genuine. So what the hell!

The biting, freezing, cold, early morning air offered me little in the way of a friendly invitation. Pulling up my coat collar around my neck as I gathered my bearings, trying to shrug off the whisky swilling around inside me, I walked over to the terminal to ask directions to the train station. A friendly security guard pointed me to the taxi rank outside telling me that 'Catching a cab' was the best option available to get me to the train station fast. Enough time to warm up with a couple of coffees before boarding the train for the twenty-minute journey into the city centre, and allowing me time to come up with my next plan, which was to find a reasonable hotel or boarding house before sussing out a few bars, picking up information as to what time and where the funeral was taking place.

There was already a sizeable queue of people waiting at the taxi rank, huddled in their coats, hands in pockets, like a bunch of homeless refugees waiting for the relief bus to arrive. As I

took my place at the end of the queue, expecting to be standing there a good half hour or so, seeing as there wasn't a single taxi in sight anywhere. I stood there, stamping the ground with my feet, trying to keep warm. Looking forward to finding a nice, cosy, traditional Irish bar with a roaring log fire crackling away, where I could sit and thaw out over two or three hot toddies.
In all the years spent living and working in Ireland, I'd never visited Belfast, apart from one memorable, distinctly, uncomfortable December night, two days' before Christmas with Karen. We were driving up from Galway to catch the ferry home to Blackpool for the festivities, looking forward to seeing friends and family for a few days. From the moment we left Galway the roads were jam packed the whole journey north, making progress painfully slow. To the point where I seriously thought that we'd miss the ferry, which meant we'd be facing a long drive back to Galway. Part of this was due to the less than brilliant navigating skills of my drunken navigator, as we somehow found ourselves in central Belfast hopelessly lost and searching for some sign to show us the way to the ferry terminal.

To me, Belfast had always been a place I looked on as dark and forbidding because of 'the Troubles' that had torn the city and its inhabitants apart for decades and no other place was as symbolic of that terrible time as The Shankhill Road which was exactly the place where we found ourselves driving down when disaster occurred. The trusty old Saab starting to overheat badly, the dial reaching the red danger zone in seconds, sending me into panic mode, as the fan belt snapped and we glided to a stop outside a pub. With only an hour and a half remaining for us to catch the ferry in good time - What to do, where to go, and who to ask, flashed through my mind - Feeling like I was about to pass out in panic, as the reality of our situation kicked in, knowing that we couldn't have broken down in a worse place.

Two Brit's in a car with English number plates, it was about as dangerous as I imagined it could get. With Karen well and truly out of the game, as far as offering me a hand to get us back on the road was concerned. Solving our dilemma was going to lie firmly and squarely on my shoulders. As I flicked an imaginary coin in my brain, wondering what to do next. Heads I walk into a Catholic pub; tails I walk into a Protestant pub. Either one didn't exactly fill me with a Colgate ring of confidence, as I jumped out of the car, opened the bonnet and stood there for a couple of minutes staring at the engine clueless as to what to do next. Whilst plucking up the courage to make a move, before we lost all hope of spending Christmas in Blackpool, to face a long hard drive back to Galway.

Thankfully, as if from nowhere, I didn't have to do anything. Two men approached me asking 'If I was having any trouble?' In that harsh, unmistakable, guttural Belfast accent, with me wondering if I was going to end up with a bullet in the back of my head. I explained the mess I was in to both of them. The older of the two men pulled out his mobile, grinning at me as he dialled a number telling me 'No worries there big man, I'll have this little problem fixed in no time at all, so I will.'

He asked his friend Terry to escort us over to the pub, where we could get a drink and warm our frozen bones, which sounded like a fine idea as far as I was concerned. Waking Karen up, dragging her out of the car to her feet, as we walked over to the pub, which was packed out with early Christmas revellers all having a blinding time. As I got a round in, three large whiskies one for Terry, which he accepted with a nod and a smile, wishing him 'All the best', whilst taking a seat by the huge roaring open fire.

'And the same to you too, Pete boy, we'll have ye' on the ferryboat back to Blackpool before ye' know it so we will.'

True to his word, Terry's friend Fergal walked into the bar about an hour later, all smiles and promises of a job completed, telling me that we were ready to go as soon as we liked; refusing point blank to take a penny for his labours, apart from the cost of a new fan belt, some radiator sealant and a bottle of anti-freeze. As I got the whiskies in for a much appreciated goodbye drink for the lads, before shaking hands never to see one another ever again and wishing them both a very Happy Christmas and New Year. With me staggering slightly out of the pub, feeling a tad worse for wear, looking forward to crashing down in the cabin for the night. As well as leaving me with one important lesson in life, I'd forgotten over and over again through the years. Never ever judge a book, or in this case two books, by their covers.

Breaking down in Belfast that night brought to mind a similar occasion I experienced with Karen, during another one of her drinking binges. We'd arrived in Dublin on a cold windy night and I was doing my best to find the N17, the main road to Galway. With Karen sitting they're shouting and screaming at me enjoying the fact that I was running out of patience. Finally enough was enough, so I swerved over to the hard shoulder, with my temper having gone past boiling point, and after punching the windscreen hard, out it popped, and then caught by the wind a fraction of a second later smashing it to pieces on the other side of the road. At that moment the heavens opened up with a vengeance, 'cats and dogs' teeming down from the sky as Karen sat there cackling away, loving the moment. I switched the engine and the windscreen wipers on, and slipped onto the N17 and drove all the way to Galway with the wind flapping my cheeks, feeling like I was in a Lancaster bomber trying to make it home on two engines. Karen by then curled up in the foot-well thinking I'd lost the plot. Calling me every name under the sun, as I tuned up the music and guess what CD? The Waterboys album This Is The Sea of course. Priceless!

And there I was back in Belfast for the second time in five years. Wondering how long I'd have to wait freezing to death, before a cab turned up to take me to the station, when a familiar face distracted my thoughts. Shouting and waving at me sitting behind the wheel of a car, nothing like the Bentley he'd arrived in back in Heysham. Instead he was driving a battered, faded, rusty, twenty plus year old maroon Volkswagen Polo minus its hubcaps.

'Well don't just stand there, Pete lad. Jump in and I'll give you a lift.' He shouted an offer that was music to my ears. I dropped my bag in the boot and slipped into the seat beside him. 'Cheers Bob, much appreciated mate. I thought I was never going to get a cab today', I replied. With Bob wasting no time at all getting out of Larne and on to the main road into Belfast City Centre which was already building up with an unusually large convoy of traffic, no doubt there for the same reasons we were.

'Yeah tell me about it Pete. It's going to be bloody impossible to get in, or out of Belfast tomorrow. It looks like the worlds turning up to see Georgie off.'

The old Volkswagen's interior was as rough as it was from the outside, but something Bob appeared to be totally unconcerned about, as he turned up the volume of a Best of Dusty Springfield CD, adjusted his seat as far back as possible, and settled down for the high speed drive to the City Centre. Explaining to me why he was driving a wreck of a car and pre-empting my question.

'Well Pete, the reason I drive this heap of crap around is because it gives me the perfect camouflage. I've been living and working in Belfast on and off for over thirty years, all told. And due to the nature of the work I do, well not so much these days now we've seen the end of 'the Troubles', but back in the 70's and 80's when there was so much violence occurring on the streets of Belfast on a daily basis, I quickly learned that the less attention I brought to myself, the more I was able to blend into the background and the more chance I'd have of staying alive. That I wasn't going to be blown to bits every time I switched the engine on, and to date, fingers crossed, the plans worked out fine. Something that wouldn't have happened if I'd been seen driving around here, there and everywhere, in a posh Bentley with private UK number plates.' Bob once again read my mind, knowing what my next question to him was going to be which was what'd he'd actually done as a job in Belfast for so long? As he explained to me the truth and nothing but, how he'd decided to make the move from Manchester, to one of the most dangerous cities in the world back then.

From the moment he'd arrived in his new home, a young, talented, idealistic advocate, determined to make his own impact on the escalating violence, Bob knew all too well that he was a potential target every time he left his house every morning. A non-descript, old red brick terraced house, situated in the dangerous labyrinth of cramped streets in and around the Shankhill Road, where much of the violence took place on a daily basis.

Furnished with only the bare minimum of life's luxuries, with a cramped upstairs room he used as a makeshift legal office. Returning home every night with take away food, fish and chips or a pizza, washed down with a few cold cans and a couple of whisky night-caps to help him forget the dangers of another day.

'Without a word of lie, I had more bloody disguises than the Scarlet Pimpernel. Long hair, short hair, beards and moustaches, you name it, and I grew it. But that's the way it was back then, and a small price to pay for maintaining my normal image in the community. The sound of gunfire and bombs exploding all over the bloody place, while I prepared my various cases for those suspected of carrying out terrorist attacks upstairs in the old bedroom. More and more Catholics were shipped out to quieter parts of the country, fearing for their lives and home, while others were housed on council estates on the city's outskirts. Places like the Cregagh estate, where I lived for a brief time, started to get really heavy for me living where I was. In fact, you won't know this, Pete lad, but I lived on the estate where George Best grew up. In fact, if you aren't doing anything special? I'll show you the house where he lived. They've done it up a lot over the years, but back then it was a pretty scary place to live. But unlike other similar council estates on the Cregagh, Catholics mixed with their Protestant neighbours with no problems at all.'

'For an all too brief time, peace and harmony prevailed and the two communities even joined forces to form the Cregagh Tenants Association in a bid to keep the estate free of violence and drugs and they were doing fine, until the Ulster Defence Association moved in to police the area. They were a right bunch of evil bastards that lot, clamping down on any of their own mixing with the Catholics, even going to the lengths of torturing their own kind to keep them separate. I take it you've heard of The Shankhill Butchers?' Bob asked me.

I nodded a definite yes to his question, after reading a book about them a few years back. Before he went on to describe to me in graphic detail just why the mere mention of their name would strike terror and fear into any person unfortunate enough to fall into their murderous clutches. From 1975 to 1982 a small group of men from the vehemently loyalist Ulster Volunteer Force took violence to a previously unprecedented level. Calling themselves 'The Shankhill Butchers', their gruesome exploits

were written about in all the gory details, in a book of the same name by Martin Dillons. The self styled leader of the gang was a dedicated loyalist called Lenny Murphy, who revelled in the violence and torture he inflicted on his many victims. Lenny and his boys operated in pubs like the Windsor Bar and the Brown Bar, in and around the loyalist stronghold of the Shankhill Road. As well as the infamous Nissen hut like building called the Lawnbrook Social Club. Where they carried out countless acts of torture and murder after which, many of their victims were found naked and badly mutilated with their throats cut.
The gang also boasted several women, who were just as cruel and bloodthirsty as their male colleagues. Operating from what were called 'romper rooms', highly secret holding places were their victims were kept alive for days; repeatedly beaten and tortured, before they were finally put out of their misery.

'I'm telling you Pete. The whole thing was total bloody insanity from start to finish. Internment, the Hunger Strikes, Sunday Bloody Sunday, when the Para's shot over a dozen Catholic peace marchers to death! Most of them shot in the back. They became the most hated regiment in the British army because of what they did that day, and despite the overwhelming evidence that they'd committed a massacre, nobody who was there and had taken part was ever prosecuted. As expected, the Lord Widgery inquiry found the army 'Not Guilty', that they were fired on first. But the whole of Belfast thought otherwise. As a result of 'Bloody Sunday', hundreds of young Irish lads flocked to join the IRA, swearing to avenge the deaths. And that's why 'the Troubles' lasted so much longer than they should have. Religion! Who the bloody hell needs it 'eh?'

Bob certainly knew his way around Belfast, weaving in and out of the traffic with the effortless touch and courage of a seasoned professional rally driver, as we hit the A12 ring road. After which he insisted on taking me on a whirlwind sightseeing tour of all the old infamous hotspots that will forever be synonymous with 'the Troubles', where Catholics fought with Protestants, with the British army wedged in between the warring factions, trying to maintain law and order in a nightmare, urban theatre of war of cramped streets, terraced houses and sprawling council estates. Knowing that around every new corner imminent danger was waiting for them, be it a bullet, or a bomb, which in turn gave me a healthy respect for my cheerful wise chauffeur. Trying to get my head around how he'd managed to survive in one piece, waking up to all that madness and murder every day.

The Andersonstown Estate, The Falls, Crumlin, Shankhill Road, and the sinister inhospitable mass of concrete called the Divis flats. Where quite a number of young, nervous, unsuspecting squaddies out on another nights patrol, met their deaths. Courtesy of the Brit hating residents, dropping fridges, televisions, dishwashers and concrete paving slabs on the heads of the unsuspecting soldiers.

'It was a constant living daily nightmare Pete! With so many young people wasting their lives caught up in the never ending violence, all for the cause of religion. Just as the world is doing as we speak, with no end in sight. It's a comforting thought knowing that George Best was born in 1946 and was signed up to play for United six years before 'the Troubles' began. Ten years later, and I'm telling you, it could have been an entirely different story. He'd have been living in Belfast when 'the Troubles' kicked off, like so many other teenagers were back then. I often think thank God he was born when he was, and what might have happened to him? What path he would have gone down and what side of the sectarian fence he'd have chosen if he'd have been born a decade later? Where his loyalties would have lain, and would he have been willing to lay down his life for his chosen course? Like I'd watched so many headstrong lads do, caught up in the cycle of increasing violence. I mean can you imagine it, the possibility of the world deprived of watching George Best play football?'

To be brutally honest, listening to Bob pouring his heart out to me that afternoon, I'd never given any serious thought to 'the Troubles' and what was actually happening in Belfast every day. I'd reached adolescence and was well into football, booze, birds, drugs, scooters and Northern Soul, like Bob had been a decade earlier. Sure, I watched all the news reports on the television, featuring what was going on across the water, but it might as well have been Mozambique for all I cared back then. But what Bob described to me and showed me that Friday, really hit home, like never before. What living through all that pointless violence must have been like for those facing it every day of their lives? A real bloody war fought between the British army and the Irish Republican Army. One of the most professional and toughened terrorist groups in the world! A fanatical bunch of men, far removed from the misconception that they were only a bunch of ill disciplined 'potato farmers', facing the centuries old military experience of the mighty British army who would destroy the IRA in a matter of weeks. Just as the Americans had boasted about smashing the Vietnamese army in over ten years, years spent fighting a pointless and costly war, before fleeing from the rooftop of the American embassy in helicopters leaving hundreds of people behind to suffer 'a fate worse than death' for their part in helping the capitalist invaders.

Bob was absolutely spot on talking about George Best being born at the right time, and that he possessed an extraordinary natural talent he'd developed as a kid. Dreaming one day of playing professional football for Manchester United, who in turn warranted enough interest in him to sign him up, and bring him to Old Trafford to begin his career. Quite simply put, there would have been no George Best as the world came to know him. He may well have been another pointless victim of 'the Troubles', and we'd have all been oblivious to the life and death of the promising young 'Belfast Boy.' And how tragic would that have been for all true football fans the world over? My immensely knowledgeable guide's impromptu tour around the epicentre of sectarianism gave me much food for thought, as to what the innocent civilians of Belfast had to cope with in their lives.

'And all in the name of the lord.' Bob concluded.

But there was one more surprise he had up his sleeve, which he was saving for last as he pulled on to the Cregagh council estate just sitting there smiling away to himself looking like he was the cat who'd just got the cream. Leaving me sitting next to him wondering why? He slowed the car down to a slow crawl up a road called the Burren Way, where unusually large crowds of people on both sides of the road had gathered. Some stood silently together, while others were just standing around talking between themselves, the majority wearing Manchester United scarves and shirts, reminiscent of so many scenes witnessed outside Old Trafford; the crowd waiting patiently for the gates to open, discussing the game and what they were about to witness.

A much larger crowd had gathered outside a house at the top of the road. Sullen faced men and women of all ages, young and old, stood like there was an oppressive cloud of doom and gloom hanging above them, and to all intents and purposes there was. Bob explained to me that the house, number sixteen Burren Way, was where a young George had grown up before United enticed him away from the security of his home and family.

A mass of floral tributes, football scarves, and shirts covered the small front garden. All donated by fans of all clubs there to pay respect to the 'Belfast Boy.' The house was a complete surprise to me, not that I expected grandeur in any way shape or form. Just an average, neat, ordinary, semi-detached standard Government Issue council house box, with a distinct difference to all the others on the estate, because of the fact it was where George had once lived. Leaving for school every morning before returning home to swap his tedious homework chores for the much more enjoyable pursuit of a kick about on the rolling green park, opposite the Best family pile. Mad childhood twenty a side matches lasting hours on end, until they wore themselves out or their parents called time on their fun. Cocoa and pyjamas and a kiss on the cheek as they snuggled down to sleep, dreaming of returning to the pitch to settle the score in another 'do or die' struggle.

Rough and tumble kids playing their hearts out screaming for a pass. Frantically charging after the ball with the enemy in hot pursuit, like the ill fated Light Brigade charging full tilt to death and destruction via the Russian artillery, positioned either side above the valley of death.

The uneven playing fields of the Cregagh, was where one very special kid in particular, discovered his talent for running rings around his friends, slamming in goal after goal in matches ending in ridiculous scores forty-eight to twenty two. Dark sets in once again forcing the game to be abandoned until the following evening. Hundreds of lonely, solitary hours spent banging a ball against back alley walls and gates. Moulding both his feet to every little touch of the ball until he was satisfied he'd mastered everything he needed to. Performing spellbinding tricks, he would replicate in football stadiums all over the world, leaving crowds stunned and amazed by his talent. The tough, uncompromising, Cregagh Estate was where George Best the footballer was born; a bright kid, who didn't want anything else in life to get in the way of achieving the impossible dream of playing professional football for a living.

Working class Cregagh council kids' didn't have too many career options open to them; The army, an apprenticeship surrounded by the noise and sweat in the mighty Harland and Wolfe shipyard where the magnificent albeit ill-fated Titanic was built, or a carpenter or bricklayer in the building industry. Maybe a clutch of the more academically gifted kids making it to college and university to study for a secure, well paid, professional career in law, medicine or architecture.

By all accounts young George was no slouch. As a kid he won a place at a local grammar school, where to his horror he discovered that rugby took precedent over football on the school curriculum. At the time he looked nothing more than a small, fragile, skinny waif of a kid, hardly suited for the rough and tumble rigours of playing rugby. So it was no surprise to his parents when he told them he desperately wanted out of the new school, and a quick return to his old one. Where he could be around his mates and pick up on his love of football once again. There were no schools, colleges or universities offering careers in professional football, which meant that George was going to have to do it all, off his own bat. Practicing for endless, uncertain hours, honing the skills that would eventually take him to 'fame and fortune' after leaving the playing fields and back alleys of the Cregagh. No guarantees on offer and with all the odds stacked against him in achieving his dream, as he blocked out the probable reality of failure choosing instead to concentrate on his all consuming dream of making the big time. And let's face it, without the dreams we dream, no matter how simple or impossible they are, what is the purpose of this ball of fun we call life?

From what I could see, it looked to me like the large crowd gathered outside number sixteen Burren Way was there for the duration. A sombre, silent, midnight vigil as Bob inched the old Polo in between the people and out of the estate. Driving for some ten minutes down a labyrinth of streets, suddenly stopping outside a similar house to all the others on the estate, turning to me smiling as he switched off the engine.
'Well Pete, here we are 'home sweet home', so to speak. So grab your case and come on in and make yourself at home. I've got a couple of bottles of special reserve Glenfiddich that I've been waiting to crack open, and there's no finer moment to do that.'

Bob may well have been one hell of an accomplished, courageous, legal advocate, but his interior design skills left a lot to be desired. But as I was all too aware having never quite found the time to fix the sores in my life that needed urgent attention, one has to take care of the 'bread and butter' issues needed to survive from day to day and all the rest. Well there's always another day. Bob's Belfast pile was basic, small and cosy, but not in a cramped way. Downstairs was a lounge with bare timber floors and emulsion walls. There were two Chesterfields surrounding a coffee table and a larger cabinet, on which was perched a large, shiny, black, state of the art digital television next to a micro CD system. Shelves were crammed with CD's, DVD's and paperback books, including a set of novels by one of my favourite authors Philip Kerr and an impressive leather bound collected works' of Ernest Hemingway. A writer I always reached for whenever I feel like a bit of excitement and danger in far off places.

The Spartan, simplistic theme continued through to the antiquated kitchen. With a large chrome Gaggia coffee machine that stood out like a sore thumb, simply because of its shiny size, an old, white enamelled Canon gas cooker, stood next to a small stainless steel sink unit evoking fleeting memories of happy childhood times watching my mum standing over an identical cooker to Bob's model which she kept cleaner than the day the friendly man from the gas board delivered it. I remember her standing over it countless times, checking on the state of the Sunday roast beef dinner with all the trimmings, followed by her special home made creamy milk pudding, covered by a thin, crispy, brown skin with a dollop of Robinson's strawberry jam in the middle - Happy days!

Bob grabbed the bottle of Glenfiddich, handing me an expensive, intricately engraved, lead crystal Waterford whisky tumbler. He instructed me to follow him through to the lounge, where I flopped down on one of the faded green leather Chesterfields, as Bob set about organising the entertainment, leaving me to do the honours pouring out two generous measures of the prize amber nectar, watching him slip a DVD compilation of some of George Best's finest goals into the player, accompanied by Van Morrison's Philosophers Stone album, which hit the spot.

We both settled down, shoes off, feet up, watching the classic footage of George weaving his unique magic on the green baize, and in between the magic, Bob showing me a photograph of his main home, a sprawling, old, isolated, sandstone farmhouse nestled in the Cumbrian hills, with the market town of Kirkby Stephen only a ten minute drive away. The house was spectacular in every way, leaving me quietly impressed listening to Bob describing it to me. His very own secret sanctuary, far from the madding crowd, where he could hide away in seclusion and recharge his batteries when the pressures of life weighed too heavy on his tired, aging, shoulders.

Two large ones later, feeling like I could sleep forever and a day, it was getting late and I needed to make a move now if I stood any chance of finding a hotel room for the night, when Bob suddenly announced an idea that was music to my ears.

'I don't want to sound like I'm encroaching on your time, Pete lad, but seeing as it's getting late and rather cold out there, by the looks of it. Why don't you stay here for the night? I've a bed made up in the spare room, okay it's not much, but it will be a dam sight warmer than marching around Belfast looking for a hotel or bed and breakfast that isn't fully booked. You can get your head down and get good nights kip, and grab a nice hot shower tomorrow morning before we set off for the funeral. What do you say? Because if it's a yes, I don't know about you, but I'm bloody famished now. So how about I order us up some grub from the Indian, while you crack open another bottle of whisky?'

'Yeah go on then Bob, thanks for the offer mate much appreciated. But on one condition, you let me take care of the bill for the grub?' I told him as he pulled out his mobile with a grin and dialled up the pleasant sounding man from Bombay down the end of the line who took the order, and what an order! A creamy vibrant chicken tikka massala, a hot spicy lamb jalfrezi with pilau and vegetable rice, onion bhajis, nan bread, tarka dahl and a colourful assortment of pickles which went down a real treat easily ranking as one of the most delicious

Indian banquets I've ever eaten. Both of us sprawled out on the Chesterfields stuffed to the gills, seconds away from slipping into unconsciousness. We shared out what remained of the second bottle of Glenfiddich, as Bob declared that it would be criminal to leave such a fine drop half empty. I agreed, raising my glass to his with a toast.

'To Georgie, and let's hope he has a good one Pete.'

'Here's to tomorrow Bob, for George.'

'Come on, down the hatch before we bugger off to bed. I dunno about you? But I'm pissed as a fart now and the last thing I need when I wake up tomorrow is a bloody hang over.'

Wise words indeed, which is exactly what I woke up with the following morning, the final whisky of the evening had finished me off big time waking up shocked and fully clothed in one of those 'where the fuck am I?' panics; in a strange room with no carpet and faded rough plastered yellow matt walls. My mouth and tongue fur lined and dry, while a battery of carnival drummers banged out a loud rhythmic samba beat in what was left of my brain, forcing me to make one of my now or never moves, knowing that if I didn't I'd be well and truly out for the count for the rest of the day. I summoned up what strength remained and slowly rose from the bed Bella Lugosi style, trying to find my bearings through puffy half closed eyes stuck together with a portion of nights sleep. One foot on the floor, followed by the other, over to my bag rummaging around to find my emergency hang over cure, I've used countless times in so many identical desperate situations in order to save the day.

Twenty minutes later, sprawled out on the leather Chesterfield having swallowed six Codeine washed down with two large hot toddies laced with plenty of sugar, I was feeling loads better waiting for my life support system to fully kick in. I must have drifted off into a deep forty winks, because the next thing I was conscious of was of Bob standing over me with a plate of sizzling bacon barms, urging me to eat some breakfast and get a move on before the crowds arrived, depriving us of a decent view of the funeral cortege.

Within an hour, we were feeling and looking loads better. Watching the morning news reporter announce that 'The funeral of football legend George Best was being held in Belfast today, where thousands of well wishers were expected to flood into the city to pay their final respects to one of the cities much loved sons.' As it turned out, the news reporter wasn't wrong. As the sudden emotion of what was to come almost got the better of us. Sitting there, hair slicked back, dressed in standard funeral issue black and white, looking like a couple of MIB's about to undertake a new mission tracking down alien invaders. As Bob leaned over and poured out a large shot.

'Why don't we have a final one for the road, eh Pete?'

'Yeah go on then Bob, why the hell not!'

SEVEN

'Yeah man the 60's was a real gas, but I'm telling you, if you remember it, then you weren't really there.' Whenever the subject of the 60's rises to the conversational fore, I've forgotten how many meaningless, boring, dinner parties I've sat through listening to so called 'hip' people, too young to have been there, raving on about how wonderful it was and how it changed America and Britain forever without a shot ever being fired, to the point where I almost spewed up my Black Forest gateau all over the table.

Inspired by the 'Turn on, tune in and drop out' immortal words spoken by the famous psychedelic adventurer Timothy Leary. Followers of the hedonistic mind expanding Camelot really did believe that they were going to change the world. But for America as the clock struck one second passed midnight, signalling the end of the 60's and welcoming in the 70's, the original 60's hippy, sex, love, rock and roll dream had turned into a nightmare. For most of the decade the world's greatest superpower and self appointed global guardians of democracy and free speech, was a country torn apart by constant internal trouble and strife. In Dallas on November 22nd, 1963, John F Kennedy the one man who could have changed the face of world politics, and in the process making him the greatest American President who ever lived was assassinated by Lee Harvey Oswald. His younger brother Bobby would suffer the same fate on June 5th, 1968 when a Palestinian Sirhan Sirhan shot him in the Ambassador Hotel in Los Angeles.

In many former Confederate Southern States, violent race riots between red-neck whites and Black Americans; sick of being treated as second class citizens, exploded, with the police and the National Guard mercilessly attacking Blacks, beating them unconscious before dragging them off to the waiting wagons. No longer willing to tolerate the racist segregation 'white bars only' and school bus policies, determined black militants joined the Nation of Islam dedicated to fighting for their rights to equality. Their leader was a man called Malcolm X, who himself was assassinated by three of the Nations' own members in February 1965, because of the rumours spreading around the brothers that he was 'Not as passionate and committed to the equal rights cause as he should have been' considering he was the founding leader!

Martin Luther King - the man dedicated to the cause of black equality through peaceful means; was the black nations' greatest spokesman of his time. Respected and loved by all colours, the man who will forever be remembered in history as the organiser of the greatest civil rights march in American history, when whites stood shoulder to shoulder with their black brothers listening to his immortal 'I had a dream speech.' Martin Luther King possessed the same unique human charisma and vision of a peaceful future JFK had, and sadly suffered the same fate. He was assassinated on April 4th, 1968, in Memphis Tennessee.

Clearly the country was in deep turmoil, heightened by America fighting a war it was never going to win in the jungles and rice fields of Vietnam, where the overwhelming technologically superior American military machine was given a nightmare lesson in ideological guerrilla warfare, administered by the tough, fanatical, North Vietnamese peasant army against young, inexperienced, American soldiers. Experiencing their first, and for many their last, tour of duty and fed on political bullshit that they were fighting the war for democracy and the American way of life, they were trapped in a constant nightmare, praying they would return home in one piece, from the second their helicopters landed on the red dusty soil of Vietnam. Meanwhile as the soldiers lay in their sandbagged dug outs getting high on dope, acid and speed, trying to forget the nightmare reality surrounding them every day, desperately dreaming of their folks and friends back home, the peace movement dedicated to opposing and bringing the war to an end was rapidly growing in popularity. On University Campuses all across the country, anti-war demonstrators clashed with police and National Guard. Ripping up their draft cards and refusing to be conscripted into fighting an enemy thousands of miles away from home they saw as 'no threat whatsoever to America.'

Soldiers returning home fully expecting a heroes' welcome, were bitterly disappointed at finding themselves shunned by the people they thought they were protecting. Looked on by many as merely 'stupid expendable puppets' manipulated by the strings of the misguided foreign policy and the mighty American propaganda machine. Many soldiers never recovered from the experience. Social outcasts who thought they were doing their bit for President and Country turned to drugs, booze and crime to help them cope with the anger raging inside caused by societies rejection.

At the height of the insanity, a magical moment occurred that offered momentary hope and optimism for a more peaceful world. In August 1969, some four hundred thousand people gathered in a field close to the town of Bethel, outside New York. All there to be part of the now legendary 'Woodstock Festival' the greatest rock, folk music event of its time, which embodied in every way the original 'summer of love', wild, free, sex n' love, psychedelic, hippy lifestyle. But as the acid purple haze evaporated into thin air, exhausted tripped out festival goers making their way home knew that the writing was on the wall, in large luminous day-glow letters. As the 60's finally came to an end in direct contrast to how the beautiful, innocent, alternative dream began.

In the Altamont speedway stadium on December 6th, 1969, close to five hundred thousand people attended a rock concert performed by The Rolling Stones. It started out on a high note, before degenerating into indescribable madness and mayhem. Feeling the need to hire some serious security to protect them, Mick and the boys hired a chapter of the notorious 'Hells Angels' motorcycle gang, famous for their violent drink and drugs alternative lifestyle. And during the concert they certainly lived up to their reputation. As the Stones settled into their set, a man in the audience called Meredith Hunter was clearly seen to pull out a revolver intending to shoot Jagger. As he took aim, one of the 'Hells Angels' named Alan Passaro noticed this and sprang into action. Pulling out his knife, he repeatedly stabbed Hunter to death with a vengeance in a bid to protect the Stones. Panic ensued and the images of the 'Hell's Angels' storming the stage forming a protective ring around the band, is one of the most iconic images in film history, providing a sad and crazy end to a decade that offered so much, to so many.

In stark comparison to the 60's America experienced, the British alternative was a far happier, optimistic, creative and fun decade for all, and we have one momentous moment in English social history to thank for this. Under the leadership of the Harold Macmillan Government conscription was finally abolished for the first time in our Island's history. Whereas American youth were fighting and dying in Vietnam, British youth were no longer forced to join the armed services, to go to fight and die in distant lands for King (or Queen) and Country.

The only wars our young people were fighting were against one another; Mods battling with Rockers on Brighton beach, later immortalised in the classic youth cult film Quadrophenia, and Skinheads battling with Teddy Boys and pretty much anyone who fancied a fight, in seaside resorts as: Margate, Hastings, Clacton and Southend on Sea.

The cost of winning the Second World War had crippled Britain almost beyond recovery. For over a decade austerity was a byword for life in Britain, but there was light at the end of a very dark tunnel and as the country slowly managed to crawl back onto its feet, the advent of the 60's heralded a brand new beginning. New opportunities created new jobs that in turn created new money and allowed British youth, for the first time in history, to stamp their brand new, clearly defined identity on society; much to the chagrin of the po-faced establishment responsible for running the countries affairs for centuries.

Swinging 60's London rapidly became the innovative, vibrant, trendsetting epicentre of the world, creating its own style and image that is as relevant today, as it was back then. British manufacturing and engineering industries led the world in design and quality. The Concorde, arguably the world's most beautiful aircraft after the Spitfire, surpassed all previous aeronautical achievements, with its ability to fly passengers in luxury at supersonic speeds. Triumph, Norton, BSA and Matchless turned out the best of home grown motorcycle designs sought after classics by bike collectors the world over. The iconic Mini offered cheap, trendy, fun motoring to the masses, while for around two thousand pounds, you could get behind the wheel of two more iconic examples of 60's car design that offered owners unparalleled quality and opulence for their money. I'm talking about Jaguar's classic Mark Two four door saloon and the super, sexy, streamlined E Type. Both cars featured all leather interiors, manual or automatic gearbox, chrome wire wheels and numerous engine options, offering ordinary people the chance to own cars oozing the kind of opulence and style normally reserved for well-heeled celebrities, cabinet ministers, and that other seemingly sixties phenomenon - gangsters.

A Frenchman by the name of Andre Courreges may well have been the man responsible for designing the mini skirt; the greatest female fashion statement of the 60's, but it took the business skills and marketing vision of Mary Quant, the British fashion designer, working in conjunction with models like 'Twiggy', to take it from the drawing board to the high streets of towns, cities and villages nationwide. It became an instant 'must have' wardrobe accessory, every young fashion conscious 'girl about town' could not risk being without. Much to the disgust of parents and older people, who viewed the sight of so many near naked legs as subversive and immoral.

Norman Foster and Eric Bedford were instrumental players in designing the new style of architecture. While David Hicks and Habitat furniture store founder Terence Conran, produced cheap, stylish, modern furniture to compliment this new style. With money and mobility at their disposal, young peoples' leisure tastes became more sophisticated, changing almost as fast as their fashion tastes.

The Spanish package holiday phenomenon was taking off big time. While romantic candlelit dinners, sipping bottles of Le Piat D'or in a favourite Italian, Indian or Chinese restaurants became the norm, before go-go dancing the night away in one of the modern discotheques opening up all over the country that were replacing the faded Victorian ballroom décor with flashing strobe lights and disco glitter balls.

The Beatles, Stones, The Who and Small Faces became the new music world ambassadors. While the British film industry was booming, boasting a formidable collection of fresh diverse talented actors who starred in ground breaking controversial films that questioned many outdated social sexual and moral issues. Film such as: Saturday Night Sunday Morning, Villain, Performance, The Servant and Blow Up. Michael Caine, Oliver Reed, Richard Harris, Terence Stamp, David Hemmings, James Fox, Albert Finney, Dirk Bogarde, Richard Burton, James Mason, Sean Connery, Glenda Jackson, Elizabeth Taylor, Rita Tushingham, Susan George, Julie Christie, Sarah Miles, Charlotte Rampling. All 'larger than life' actors and actresses, who will be forever synonymous with the British 60's film industry. Without doubt, Britain was a country on the move. Experiencing a bloodless, nationwide revolution; that changed the social fabric of the country forever. To the disgust of the time honoured establishment, who hated the changing times.

But not everyone joined in with the change, like footballers' for example, who for various reasons seemed impervious to what was going on before their very eyes. Many of them were of the older generation set in their ways, who'd seen action in the Second World War and survived to live another day. They believed in the old social order, duty to King or Queen and Country, ready to tug their forelock in recognition of those in power. Their image was stiff, neat, tidy, short back and sides, traditionally dressed, conservative veneer backed up by an old fashioned outdated Roy of the Rovers, 'I say, Sir play up and play the game, and may the best man win, of course Sir' attitude. That was the mind set of most players who played professional football for a living back then. In the 60's, football was a galaxy away from the multi billion comfortable middle class profit making global mega force it is today. Calling on the talent of home grown players' from all corners of the United Kingdom, instead of importing world talent, players didn't even know how to spell the word Lamborghini, never mind own one! Indeed many players' didn't own a car and frequently travelled by bus or train to their next fixture.

Jimmy Armfield who was the much respected captain of Blackpool and England, we used to see many times carrying his sports bag, leaving his house in Beechfield Avenue for the walk down to Bloomfield Road without a bodyguard, or an entourage of paparazzi snappers in sight. Laughing and joking with him as to who was going to win the game? For the honour and privilege of playing football week in week out, the vast majority of players' were paid a pittance; that kept them hovering just above the poverty line, meaning that they had to take a second job to help support their families from week to week. One notable example was the brilliant Tom Finney of Preston and England. A naturally friendly, down to earth bloke, who in his spare time managed to build up a thriving plumbing business in between nurturing his passion for kicking a ball around in earnest.

To keep up with the whirlwind of social change blowing through the Country's every nook and cranny, clearly the dyed in the wool traditional image of English football had to change. And change it did at three o'clock on the afternoon of 14th September, 1963, when the unlikely looking nervous young fledgling George Best made his football league debut for Manchester United against West Bromwich Albion, in front of the packed Old Trafford faithful who were more than curious to check out the new player, many people had already been talking about for weeks.

By all accounts the game was a stale, lacklustre affair, with the new player showing little of the brilliance to come, failing to score a priceless goal on his debut. George was of frail build, he was good looking with neatly styled short black hair and shirt tucked into his shorts. A conforming image he was soon to shed replaced by his trademark Beatle style long hair and thick sideburns, shirt out and socks rolled down to his ankles.

Far more important than impressing the crowd was the fact that he'd made it through his first full 'baptism of fire' without injury or incident, showing not the slightest trace of fear or a bead of sweat, totally unfazed at the prospect of playing his first game for United.

Reading through Matt Busby's autobiography and his account of that defining moment, he recalls that during his time as 'The Boss' at Manchester United, he'd witnessed a lot of top class players' in turmoil seconds before running on to the pitch to the roar of the crowd. The changing room was the place where most players' devised their own personal routines and rituals to help them cope with their twisted jangled emotions. George on the other hand, for a player so young and inexperienced, showed no nerves whatsoever, displayed no visible idiosyncrasies seconds before experiencing the greatest moment of his life at the time. He appeared ice cold, switched off, alone, and detached from the impending noise and passion, like he was born to take part in the impending drama, he always knew would happen. Thanks to the hundreds of hours he'd spent perfecting his skills on the Cregagh Estate where the United hierarchy first heard the rumours that there was a very special, bright shining star, in the making.

Two years after signing a junior contract with United, George Best's career really took off. But it could have all turned out so differently, had it not been for the wisdom and belief Matt Busby already had for his young protégé, and the support and understanding from the woman who turned out to be his surrogate mother through the early tender part of his career. George's family were fairly ordinary typical Belfast working class people, meaning there was little or no spare money left over in the purse for luxuries such as holidays. George had never been out of Belfast properly, but shortly after signing for United; along with his friend Eric McMordie another rising star, they found themselves sailing across the Irish Sea bound for Liverpool and a train journey to Manchester. Small wonder then that the two young innocents' felt scared and bewildered in the shared cabin, wondering if they'd made the right decision by leaving the love and security of their families' back home, for the unfamiliar bright lights of Manchester.

Shortly after arriving homesickness set in, prompting a quick return to Belfast for both boys. But unlike McMordie, George realised he'd made a grave mistake in turning his back on Matt Busby and Manchester United, and the prospect of becoming a professional footballer for one of the greatest clubs in the sports history just because he felt homesick; not without talking to 'The Boss' first about how he was feeling. All those childhood hours spent learning to play football were meaningless, one great big waste of time now he'd well and truly blown his chance of a ticket out of a life of sweat, toil and grime, working for peanuts in the shipyard or building site.

After talking things over with his father, common sense prevailed with George realising he'd made a mistake that he was never going to be able to recover from, and one that would haunt him for the rest of his days. Recalling in bar stories, exhausted and bitter after another thankless hard day's work, all about the time he could have made it as a professional footballer for Manchester United if only he'd have only shown more maturity and backbone. And so the prodigal son returned to Old Trafford, like he did a number of times during his career. Back to Matt Busby and Mrs Mary Fullaway with whom he lived, with her two sons in a cosy house on Aycliffe Avenue. His surrogate mother in every sense of the description, she provided George with the kind of security, support, stability and normality he badly needed during the early part of his career in a loving, down to earth environment, with home cooked food morning and night, and a nice warm bed to sleep in after relaxing in the lounge watching television for a couple of hours before an early night.

This was a time of innocence for George as Mary Fullaway strived to make his stay in her house as homely as possible. Making sure he kept in touch with his family back in Belfast as much as possible. A young, sexy footballer in the making, unaware of all the temptations lying in wait for him as his career started to blossom. The more games he played, the more exposure he attracted. The more money he earned, the more temptations were waiting to entice him from straying away from the 'straight and narrow.' Making mistakes that aren't just confined to footballers; turn over any stone and you'll find them waiting for you, whatever walk of life you hail from.

As the George Best brand blasted off into the commercial cosmos, especially after United winning the European Cup, it was inevitable that he and Mary Fullaway were bound to go their separate ways. But without the endless love and support she gave George in those crucial, uncertain, early days, it's a distinct possibility that he would not have gone on to enjoy the kind of success he attained in the game. The more popular he became, the more his life belonged to Manchester. He became the first footballing superstar symbolising everything that was cool, hip, trendy and sexy in the 60's, but it came at a terrible unforeseen price for the young player, who was the toast of Manchester. Everywhere he went, so his entourage followed, wanting to touch him, kiss him and demanding his signature. This intrusion into his private life extended to the places he liked to go: coffee bars, pubs, clubs, restaurants and cinemas. People wound down their car windows waiting for the lights to turn green, calling to him as he sat there in his distinctive white E Type Jaguar.

He co-owned two boutiques with his friend Mike Summerbee, which were packed with fans just hoping to get a glimpse, or a touch of him. The mere mention of his E Type Jag brought a grimace to Bob's face, remembering the time when George was the 'King of Manchester', the city he loved as much as his beloved Belfast. George had well and truly arrived on the social scene, which turned out to be a nightmare for all the other young trendy lads on the town trying to pull the girls of their dreams.

'Don't get me wrong Pete, it was great him being a part of our city. But how could any of us young bucks compete with him? The second he walked into a bar or a nightclub, flashing his smile at all the sexy young ladies, women just fell instantly for his good looks, his smile, his fashion sense and this air of innocence he had about him that they all found bloody irresistible. He'd only have to stare at them, or flash that smile, and they'd all melt like chocolate, hoping to be the one who was going home with George Best for the night. To be fair to him though, he never went out of his way to cause a scene or embarrass anybody. That wasn't his style. He loved women and he loved being around them, and let's face it, who doesn't when you're a young, good looking, suited and booted lad about town?'

'As luck had it, I bought myself an E Type Jag from a garage over in Wilmslow. Only mine was yellow. But that didn't stop people coming up to me, or stopping me on the road or the street, thinking I was George. Soon as I parked up near the office, people thinking it was George surrounded me. It drove me bloody mad! So in the end I flogged the car back to the garage where I bought it on a part exchange deal, for a dark blue Bristol 407. I had that for years, before I fell in love with Bentleys forever. I really loved the Jag as well, but Manchester wasn't big enough for two E Type Jags, so mine went. But I'm telling you, that period gave me an insight into what it must have been like for George going into town every day; A never-ending, absolute, bloody nightmare for him!'

As George talked about many times over the years, he made no excuse for earning and spending his money like it was 'going out fashion.' He was the world's sexiest, trendiest, most talented and highest paid English footballer, so why shouldn't he enjoy the wealth playing for United brought in? With members of the Stones, Beatles, Who and Pink Floyd treating themselves to the kind of stately homes and castles only the aristocracy could once afford. George felt the need for his own house, where he could get away from the hassle, where he could relax and entertain friends in the privacy of his own bricks and mortar.

Up until deciding on this move, George had lived the quiet, simple, loving life for many years with Mrs Fullaway's family in their small home in Chorlton cum Hardy. But as his fame grew rapidly out of control, and his fans demanded so much more of him than he could possibly give, the decision to move out to a house of his own was the one he took as much as his desire for a quiet life. Sadly even this proved impossible for him to do without attracting a crowd.

Swayed by the persuasive, futuristic ideas of trendy architect Frazer Crane that such a young, unique, modern footballer should naturally live in the most modern, state of the art designed home possible, George financed the building of the house in a leafy Cheshire suburb he called 'Que Sera' that he eventually moved into in 1970 unaware of the problems he was going to face as a result of the move.

Myself, I've always been a big fan of the clean, light, white aesthetics of modernist architecture, but Crane's design was way too 'far out there' for my taste. It went beyond modernism and looked totally out of place in the surroundings. It was constructed in the same way George's stunning modernist house in Sandbanks, when he lived there for a few years, combining white external walls and high circular boundary walls leading to a downstairs space to park the E Type, complemented by black window frames, holding vast expanses of one way glass to prevent any nosey parkers trying to get a glimpse of George at work or play. He paid somewhere close to thirty six thousand pounds for the luxurious privilege of living like a 'goldfish in a bowl.' It looked as if it had been made for the Thunderbird family.

I asked my old man to drive me out one Sunday afternoon, to check it out for myself in the summer of 1971, just to say that I've seen one of the most distinctive houses in Cheshire. And sure enough it was all that and more, with the E Type parked on the basement parking space. All the trappings afforded for such a young, talented, footballer, but as George recalled many times over the years, life in 'Que Sera' turned out to be one of his biggest mistakes! Nothing like he envisaged it would be. Even in Cheshire, he was continually hounded by hordes of fans making the pilgrimage to 'Que Sera', walking around the property like it was their own. Some even taking the liberty by setting up picnics on the lawn, unaware that George was inside, looking out at the unwanted intrusion of his most inner sanctum, that sadly never was.

Rain is a way of life when you live in Ireland, something you just have to accept and adapt to. And the sooner you do, the easier life becomes. Despite the fact it was the day of George Best's funeral, it was no different to the countless other downpour days I'd lived through, sitting in my old Saab wasting my time away, playing games on my Nokia, praying for a break in the clouds so I could start earning money again. And then, there were the lazy Sunday mornings in the kitchen, warmed by a roaring peat fire and a few hot toddies. Munching my way through a full English breakfast, staring at the rain soaked herd of forlorn looking cows huddled together under the only tree in the field to the sound of Van Morrison's Philosophers Stone. Bob sighed loudly, stepping out of the taxi paying the driver a handsome tip, staring up at the dull grey skies and the torrent of rain beating down.

'Looks like we're going to get wet, Pete lad, it's a good job I brought those brollies along. Come on we'd better get a move on. It looks like things are starting to get busy already despite the rain.'

Coat collars and brollies up, we trudged down to Burren Way. On either side people were silent and serious, some in their work clothes, others in their Sunday best.

In amongst the silent throng were the brave ones turned out wearing their Manchester United shirts, from the retro 60's, 70's style, through to the modern day emblazoned with sponsorship names that have become part and parcel of the politics and finance of the corporate industry modern game. Logo football from a whole host of companies: Hitachi, Wonga, Vodaphone, Sharp all desperate to see their names plastered all over shirts worn by today's rich and famous football superstars. In comparison, the basic no frills retro United shirts looked so much cooler, before the suits moved in to take over the game. Long sleeved, loose fitting, white round neck and cuffs, with no club badge on the chest. And the 70's distinctive United shirt with the white triangular collar, George Best wore towards the end of his Old Trafford career.

The young, the middle aged and the elderly, all battling the elements paying their respects to their 'Belfast Boy.' Kids and teenagers, who'd only ever heard stories or watched DVD compilations of goals he scored and the games he played in. There were people like me, who were thankfully young enough to have been privileged to see him play in the flesh, mesmerising us all with his out-of-this-worldly skills and charisma, during his last three seasons as a Manchester United player. And then there were the old timers, Bob included, although not quite as old and stately as many others there. People who'd been good friends of the Best family, knowing his Mum and Dad; Anne and Dicky, and his two sisters; Barbara and Carol well. People the young George had delivered newspapers through the letterbox to, so that he could earn some pocket money for treats, and people who'd watched him knocking the ball about on the playing fields of the Cregagh, realising that he had something unique about him as he made mugs of his mates, as well as easily holding his own when it came to the rough and tumble tackles that left him swollen and bruised until the next big game.

Down to earth, no nonsense, working class Belfast people spending their lives toiling in the shipyards, factories, shops and building sites, earning meagre wages paid on a Friday night and gone by Monday morning. As they continued on, hoping for a better life and a brighter day, waiting on a rainbow that was going to add some colour to their mundane lives, which was never going to come. These people all knew that from an early age George Best was special. They knew that given the break he needed, he was talented and ambitious enough to escape the life sentence on the Cregagh; they were still serving. But instead of feeling jealous, they unanimously wished their son 'all the very best' to go out there where few make it, and give all those who faced him hell. In a hopeless working class world for all the people living on the estate, George was their 'Che Guevara', offering hope in a hopeless world. Bob and I didn't know it at the time standing there soaked and freezing, but according to news reports on the television and in the papers, we were part of over five thousand people gathered on the Burren Way that morning. Listening to people chattering away, telling us that his coffin was lying in the front room of the Best family home waiting to be driven off to Stormont, where a ceremony befitting a sadly missed, revered, respected, statesman had been arranged.

Watching the news shortly after my return to Lancaster, I wasn't exactly surprised to hear that somewhere close to one hundred thousand people had turned out to bid farewell to their 'Belfast Boy.' It was a special day of togetherness, solidarity and unity for one man who'd given so much. When all past bitter memories of sectarianism were put aside and both Catholics and Protestants, young and old, stood together as one. Shoulder to shoulder, with pride and dignity to honour and remember the greatest footballer in the history of 'the beautiful game.'

There was a tangible weighty sadness in the air, as the funeral cortege inched down the Burren Way. The Best family and their beloved son in a hearse, covered in floral tributes. Tears flowing from many of the mourners, while others simply stood their heads bowed biting back the emotions. Heads filled with their own personal memories, unable to accept the fact that George was on his way to his final resting place in Roselawn cemetery.

Our original plan, we'd discussed the night before, was to be there every step of the way, but because of the sheer size of the crowd, combined with the foul weather Stormont felt like a 'bridge too far.' Despite the umbrellas, we were cold and wet, getting wetter by the minute. So Bob's suggestion of finding a nice, warm, cosy bar to hole up in for the day, where we could watch the funeral in comfort with a few drinks surrounded by like minded people, seemed to be a far more sensible idea.
'Yeah that sounds good to me Bob, lead the way mate, and the first rounds on me.'

As the cortege slowly disappeared into the distance, we joined the soaking wet throng shuffling down the Burren Way while Bob figured out his bearings and where to go next; either a pub on the Shankhill Road, or one on the Falls Road. Which to be honest, I didn't like the sound of, but nevertheless Bob being Bob, convinced me to leave my worries behind and concentrate on the fact that we were going to have a great day no matter where we ended up. I couldn't help remembering that unforgettable night I broke down outside the Divis flats when two hard looking Belfast blokes helped me to get my tired old Saab back on the road, in time to catch the ferry back home to Blackpool for Christmas. And the promise I made to myself, to never ever judge a book by its cover again. Besides, I was in the safe hands of an experienced man, who knew every nook and cranny in Belfast like the back of his hand. And my confidence in Bob was proved correct only minutes after we walked into a bar on the Shankhill Road. It was jam packed with people watching the ceremony. United shirts and scarves all over the place, on the day that for once in its complex and bloody history Belfast stood stone still.

Almost immediately upon seeing Bob, we were surrounded by a mob of friendly blokes shaking hands, hugs and back-slaps, smiles and laughter.

'Great to see ya', Bob boy, you're looking well so you are. And who's the big fella with ya'?'

'Pete.'

'Pleased to meet ya' there Pete. There's an old saying round here, any friend of Bob's is a friend of ours, so take ya' coat off and make yourself at home now.'

'Aye so it is, a terrible sad day for Belfast'

'Belfast and United.'

'You're spot on there big fella, there'll never be another one like Georgie, but at least we had him for a time and we have the memories he left us all with. We'll remember him forever, so we will.'

'Here's to the one and only George Best!' The bloke called Billy shouted aloud, as he stuck a pint of Guinness in my hand. Every glass in the pub was raised to the heavens followed by a rousing 'To George Best!' The first of countless toasts washed down with Guinness and whisky, as we all stood as one watching the events of the day slowly unfold before our eyes. The massive crowd packed both sides, lining the impressive elegant driveway leading to Stormont House, watching the impressive funeral cortege flanked by a squadron of police motorcycle outriders, deliver George on time for the state ceremony. Sadness, happiness, tears and smiles from all gathered in the pub that afternoon. Knowing that in all of us watching the big screen, the legacy of George Best would live on in us all, forever and a day.

Behind the bar was a video screen playing some of his greatest moments, and the wall was carpeted with a fantastic collage of photographs depicting the life and career of George Best; from his early undiscovered life on the Cregagh waiting to be discovered, to his glory days with Manchester United. And snaps of him playing soccer in America for the San Jose Earthquakes, during the game against the Fort Lauderdale Strikers in 1981; eight years after leaving his beloved Manchester United, he scored a goal many swear as being his greatest ever, although George argued otherwise because he wasn't playing for United when he scored it.

Monochrome moments frozen in time, of a young baby faced kid and previously unseen loving family snaps and the fish and chip shop he bought his dear old Dad. And a picture of him looking like a young Elvis, hair slicked back, staring at a football standing next to his friend Eric McMordie; who'd turned down the chance to play for United and Shots of his early career, short back and sides, arms folded and smiling in perfectly posed team photographs. That became the fashion of the day, decorating the walls of every football loving kid in the country. Before growing his hair and sideburns, creating the long haired 60's Beatle image he will forever be remembered for.

Turning away from the Benfica goal at Wembley, celebrating his goal neatly slotted into the net to help United win the European Cup beating the mighty Benfica 4-1. His arm raised, smiling like he means it, blue shirt tucked out of his shorts, socks down to his ankles. Enjoying every second of the world stage he found himself on, on that glorious night back in June 1968, when he was at the peak of fitness, playing ability and charisma; leaving the football world doting on his next move.

After United ran out league division one champions and George was awarded the 'Golden Ball' for international player of the year and rightly so. February 7th, 1970, two years later, after that memorable season in the fifth round of the FA Cup, United found themselves playing away to lowly Northampton Town. The tie turned out to be the expected 'walk in the park' for United, beating Northampton 8-2 and a game made all the more memorable, because it was George Best's return to football after receiving a FA ban. He was in a mean mood that afternoon, determined to show the football leagues governing body in particular, that he was back where he belonged entertaining crowds with his skills. Admittedly, lowly Northampton were no match for United. By the time the ref blew the final whistle, George had scored six goals, on what was a great comeback performance. The picture of him smiling, standing by the goalpost catching his breath after scoring reflects that time in his career when he was 'burning the candle at both ends.' Playing harder off the pitch, than on it! Two years after the day the photo was taken, he'd leave United forever.

The pub was full to bursting and all eyes and ears glued to the television screen relaying the official Stormont ceremony to the world. As each glass of Guinness and whisky hit the required spot, the screen became more fuzzy and distorted, as the landlord decided to have a lock in. Making sure everyone involved were in there until he called time and carry on George's wake the way he would have demanded of us all; warmed by a roaring log fire, conversations filling the air. As round after round flew in from all sides, thanks to the pile of cash we'd contributed to on the bar top. Ensuring there wasn't going to be a dry throat in the house, with drinks aplenty for the young, old, unemployed and those who couldn't afford to buy into the session. All too aware that come the time doors finally opened, each of us on our long and winding way home, were all going to wake up the following morning suffering from the hangover from hell. Wondering how we'd made it into bed in one piece.

As the Stormont ceremony reached its emotional finale, and the funeral cortege began the slow journey to George's final resting place in Roselawn cemetery. The manager switched off the television and turned the music up full blast, to raise our morale, each of us raising his glass to the heavens for the umpteenth time shouting 'To George!' Making sure every person had a glass of Guinness and whisky in each hand to respond to the toast.

All of us involved in that mad session, rooted to the spot, watching the television screen in the far corner showing some of his best goals; many of which happened to be my own personal favourites. Benfica, Tottenham, Chelsea, Liverpool, Sheffield United, Northampton, West Ham and the incredible goal he scored for the Los Angeles Lakers. As well the audacious disallowed goal he scored for Northern Ireland against England, wearing the dazzling emerald green. Firstly knocking the ball out of Peter Shilton's hands and then running around him leaving him for dead, before finally effortlessly sliding the ball into the England goal before the bemused ref blew for a foul against the keeper. One of the cheekiest, most imaginative goals the renegade magician never scored. Disallowed by the rigid rules of 'fair play' the football association was built on, and that, like most of life's rules, was something George never really took seriously.

For the life of me, I couldn't then and still can't now, remember a single name from the pub that afternoon apart from the bloke they called Billy, who seemed to be the pub's main boy, for want of a better expression. After a whole day, and most of the night on the booze and with the Guinness and whisky finally getting the better of us convinced us to grab the nearest two tables by the fire and crash down to continue the party. And continue it did, accompanied by baskets full of potato wedges, chicken wings, colcannon and bowls of seafood chowder with soda bread lovingly provided by the manager. All free of charge to keep the troops well fed and ready for more drinks while we listened to Bob Geldoff, Boomtown Rats, Undertones, Thin Lizzie, Stiff Little Fingers, Fergal Sharkey, Cranberries, Enya, Sinead O'Connor, The Wolfe Tones, The Dubliners, The Pogues, Van Morrison, Christy O'Connor, Saw Doctors and Snow Patrol. Three or four hours condensed history of the best of Irish music, far into the early hours of the morning, until the landlord finally called time, with a free last round 'on the house.' Pleading with us to drink up and go on our merry way.
'For fucks sake ladies and gentlemen, you've all had a fine day and had your fill. So drink up now, and be on your way.'

The generous offer of a free last drink signalled a final mad stampede to the bar, followed by everyone throwing the drink down our necks in double time, before shaking hands, hugging, kissing and laughing ourselves stupid with Bob and me ending the moment with the few old boys he nicknamed his 'inner circle.' Men he'd become best friends with shortly after the start of 'the Troubles', Billy included, ass they stood there almost in tears, studying a tattered, torn, faded monochrome moment frozen in time of an equally old timer, not too dissimilar in looks and stature to themselves. A hard faced, craggy, unassuming old pensioner stared into the camera lens wearing a flat cap, granddad shirt, waistcoat and thick woollen trousers held up by a wide leather belt standing outside an old, dilapidated stone farmhouse. Emotionless, not a trace of a smile, almost as if the expression on his face summed up the normal, mundane, hard working class life he'd lived. Like so many others, with one monumental exception. As I asked Bob who the man was? Bob in turn staring back at me shaking his head in disbelief, for asking such a ridiculous question; a true United supporter would never have asked.

As he downed his whisky in one and proceeded to put me out my misery, much to the humorous approval of his 'inner circle' ' I Can't believe you, Pete lad, you've spent the whole weekend going on about how much of a Manchester United fan you are, and that George Best is your all time favourite footballer, and you don't know who the man in the picture is? Well to put it mildly, without that man who was called Bobby Bishop, it's a fairly safe bet to say that George Best might never have played for United. He was an absolute legend in Belfast. Loved and respected by everyone who met him. And what he did for the future of football will be remembered here in Belfast forever.'

'Bob was brought up the hard way, as were so many people like him back then in the 'Dark Age.' He worked in the shipyards most of his working life, doing what he had to do to survive. He was a loner, and he never married. Some say they never even saw him with a lady on his arm. Be that as it may, what made Bob so special was his never ending passion for football. He spent all his spare time scouting out fresh, up and coming young talent for Manchester United, whom he worked for as a scout. I only ever had the pleasure of meeting him one time, and I'll never forget the way he shook my hand like a vice crushing a piece of timber. Hands like iron, hardened after years of grafting away in the shipyard. When he wasn't grafting, he spent every available second of his spare time watching young lads playing football, hoping to spot that glimmer of talent that set them apart from the rest of the competition. Back then, Pete lad every team had their own scouts working for them for peanuts. Ordinary faceless blokes, who did what they did for the love of football and their clubs, just watching in the shadows, like the SAS planning an ambush; standing there winter and summer, sunshine and rain. Scribbling down notes about this or that particular lad, to pass on to the manager informing him they just might have found 'somebody special.'

'School games, park games, minor league boy's games, you name it! And Bob Bishop was there. Focusing on the special ones, assessing their ability, skill, passion and perception as to how they played and read the game. Trying to decide if they had what it took to go on to play for Manchester United. Who were Bob Bishop's life and soul, his reason for living and breathing so he put all his efforts and understanding of football into finding only the very best to send to Old Trafford. For fear of letting down Matt Busby, which would have meant he'd have let himself down as well. From what so many people have told me Pete. From the second Bob Bishop set eyes on George Best playing football, the hairs on the back of his neck were bristling. Knowing he was watching a young lad with a rare unique talent in the making. Far and above the conveyor belt of other young hopefuls, dreaming of one day wearing the famous United red shirt. He told people he knew, even at that early stage, that he was in the presence of greatness and that there was only one thing left to do before other scouts spotted him and snapped him up for their club.'

'As legend has it, Bob got on the phone to Matt Busby to tell him he'd found a young lad who could turn out to be the 'world's greatest footballers.' That telephone call was the catalyst for United to take Bob Bishops' word seriously. And from that moment the rest is history. As it turned out, for better for worse.'

Snatched memories of an overworked pub manager shouting 'Time please, will you all please fuck off home now!' And the familiar rhythm of my samba drummers banging the drums lodged in my brain loudly, grudgingly dragged me from my unconscious slumber, into the stark painful hangover reality of a new day. Its incessant rhythm leaving both Bob and me bruised, battered and nauseous for most of the day, as we slowly recovered from the aftermath of witnessing the funeral of George Best. Bob was on one Chesterfield and me on the other, both incapacitated like two Terra Cotta soldiers barely able to move, apart from necessary trips to the toilet and the kitchen where we quickly knocked up slices of toasted bread, covered in grilled cheese, topped with onions and tomatoes and HP brown sauce. All washed down with mugs of hot black sweet Lavazza, laced with whatever rare, expensive, malt whisky was left in the cabinet. Admittedly a cardinal sin to waste such fine single malt with hot water and filter coffee, but desperate times called for desperate measures, several of them in fact throughout our recovery. Until eventually we both felt strong enough to smarten ourselves up with a shower, shave and a change of clothes and head off into Belfast City centre for a slap up meal, over which Bob volunteered to drive me back to Larne, with plenty of time to spare so I could catch the ferry back to Heysham.

My happy home in Lancaster, dreading what sad, angry, hopeless, bitter and twisted state Karen would be in when I walked through the door. And back to the Lake District, where no doubt Farmer Jim would be on pins waiting for me to pick up from where I'd left off, hoping to complete the barn renovations before the completion date. It was a fitting finale to our brief, unforgettable, friendship. After two people starting out as strangers, attending one special day in history; those of who were there will remember forever, became friends, albeit ships passing in the night.

Bob suggested that we go all out and have a slap up meal in his favourite Belfast hotel, The Europa. The building that continued to rise out of the ground after being bombed and rebuilt over twenty times during the height of 'the Troubles.' Acting as a symbol of hope, a beacon of light, shining in a dark dangerous world, offering safer, better, times to come. The Europa was the choice for countless new hungry journalists on the prowl for as much information as they could glean about the latest assassination, bombing and trial verdict. With most of them making a beeline straight to Bob, who'd be relaxing in the bar with a couple of whiskies after another arduous day in court.

'Some of the journalists and photographers I knew when this place was jam packed with them had worked in some of the world's most dangerous hotspots. Forever holed up in hotels similar to this in The Congo, Beirut, Vietnam, Angola Bosnia and Kosovo. Some of them had lost good friends killed in the fighting, while others had been badly injured. But they still carried on doing what they loved doing. They were real mad, crazy bastards, who loved the buzz of witnessing war in all its gory detail, like Soldiers without rifles; risking everything. Adrenaline junkies hooked in the moment, willing to risk life and limb in the hope of getting that one shot that would set them up for life, with a journalist or photographer of the year award and a best selling book deal. Back then in here, the buzz was exactly the same. With all of us unaware of what the next stranger who walked into the hotel was carrying, a Kalashnikov or a nail bomb? Humans and war, Pete lad, I just don't get? I never have, and I never will. We've been doing it for thousands of bloody years, and no doubt we'll carry it on until we wipe ourselves out, when none of us are left standing to tell the tale.'

'You wouldn't recognise this place now, to what it was like back then. These days it's recognised as a top luxury international hotel attracting rich and famous people from all over the world. Even Bill Clinton stayed here a few years ago, and rates it as one of his favourite hotels. They do a bloody good steak too. So how about we crack open a bottle of bubbly, while we give the menu the once over? I don't know about you? But after that session in the Rex yesterday, I'm bloody starving.'
Looking down the menu, thinking how we were going to begin our stupendous banquet, our hopes of dining in the Europa were dashed when the headwaiter apologetically informed us that the restaurant was full to bursting with no chance whatsoever of us having a meal that night. So we gave up on the idea and finished off the weekend in Bob's old banger enjoying two giant portions of fish, chips and peas with a take-out bottle of Remy Martin to wash it all down with.

It seemed a fitting final toast to the weekend and to the memory of George Best, whose life had been so cruelly stolen from us at the age of fifty nine. Both of us proud and fortunate to have been able to be there, to honour his memory, as well as saying goodbye to him in person before sending him off to his next port of call. Sitting in the momentarily silence, remembering the man, the player he was, and the myriad of personal memories he gave each and every one of us because of how he played 'the beautiful game.'

With both of us worse for wear, I told Bob that it would be a good idea if he left the car where it was for the night, and that we both jump in separate taxis. But once again Bob, being Bob, wouldn't hear a word it. The crazy, courageous, flamboyant soul, who never placed a bet on anything labelled safe in his life. Who'd swapped a safe, well paid lifestyle of a criminal advocate in Manchester, for danger and death on a day to day basis on the Shankhill and Falls Road, told me that he'd already made his mind up and that there was nothing I could say to dissuade him from driving me to the ferry port. As we both limped over to the old Polo, slid on the seatbelts and cautiously crawled out of Belfast City centre en route to my cosy warm cabin some half an hour away, barring any head on crashes along the way. Despite our painfully slow progress, Bob maintained a fairly convincing straight line, opting to keep a steady, safe, speed behind a huge articulated lorry bound for the same place I was, rather than risk our lives and those of other people by attempting a foolish overtaking manoeuvre that could have resulted in the needless deaths of all concerned. Especially in the clapped out old banger we were travelling in.

Our time was coming to an end with each mile notched up on the speedometer, leaving me a little more emotional than usual. Meeting Bob so unexpectedly, a man who shared so many teenage memories identical to mine, a decade apart, had been a fantastic experience. Tempered with so many fascinating, horrific, life threatening daily moments he'd lived through when 'the Troubles' raged and turned Belfast into a battlefield. A bloody hateful time in the city's history that can't, and must never be forgotten. No winners and no losers, in a pointless, dirty sectarian war that claimed the lives of thousands of people: Catholics and Protestants, guilty and innocent alike.

As in all wars, the dead are dumb leaving only the survivors to tell the stories, who are getting few and far between, as they grow older. And Bob was one of them. Admitting that he'd come perilously close to being shot or blown up more than most. And there he was a survivor of 'the Troubles' from beginning to end. Laughing and joking with me, telling me how it was with a stark, down to earth honesty and philosophy. And how the hell he managed to cope every single day, waking up wondering if it was going to be his last? Who was to blame and who wasn't? Now that Ireland had finally found peace but at such a human cost. We finally reached journey's end, jumping out of the car, shaking hands, hugging each other and wishing each other all the very best. Knowing we would never meet again, but would always remember the time we stood together at George Best's funeral whenever there was mention of his name.

'Take care Bob, I've had a brilliant time mate meeting you, and thanks for everything. Putting me up and introducing me to some of your mates.' I told him ending my sentiments with a handshake and what remained inside Bob's silver hip flask urging me to knock it back as he was driving.

'Think nothing of it Pete, the feelings mutual. It's been a welcome change for me to share some enjoyable, likeminded company with someone who knows what I'm on about and what I stand for. Just make sure you look after yourself and to coin an old phrase, 'Keep the faith', Pete lad.' I laughed remembering how many thousands of times I'd heard that saying over the course of my life as I watched Bob jump into his old banger fumbling for his keys, before firing up the engine. As I shouted across to him

'You too Bob, after all, guys like us, we don't have any other option do we? Take care mate.'

EIGHT

True sporting genius is a rare indefinable gift. Leaving all of us who were fortunate enough to witness it in action, full of magical memories and moments we'll remember forever. It cannot be inherited, taught or harnessed. One simply has to accept it and leave it alone to flourish and grow in its own way, for better for worse. George Best was a true genius who changed the shape of 'the beautiful game' forever. In the same way Alex Higgins, James Hunt and Ilia Nastase changed the face of their chosen sports, men who had no other choice but to aim for the stars, while teetering on the tightrope between brilliance and despair. Determined to go out and play their sport, in their own unique way. Irrespective of the win or lose factor, because they didn't know any other way to perform.

Alex Hurricane Higgins, the wild charismatic Belfast born snooker superstar, was a true sporting genius famed for his whirlwind breaks and was the one player responsible for bringing the game of snooker to the attention of the media spotlight, transforming it from a secretive affair, into a seriously entertaining sport, watched by millions all over the world. The crowds flocked to see Alex packing out venues all across the country, watching him play his game; the only way he knew how. A former world champion, who had the world at his feet, and yet, he died a penniless, homeless, alcoholic.

James Hunt was a true sporting genius, who only ever won the formula one world championship one time. But what memories he left us all with; screaming round world circuits in his distinctive red and white Maclaren racing car. He was sexy, charismatic, good looking, fearless and courageous. James Hunt was the pin up boy of the formula one world. A swashbuckling hero of the track, who earned the nickname 'The Shunt', due to the amount of crashes he was involved in, during his all too brief racing career. Almost every person I knew back in the day owned a red and white zip up Maclaren jacket, proudly wearing them at the weekend, in the pubs and clubs hoping to pull the girls. Fiercely competitive above and beyond the norm, James Hunt also cared deeply for his fellow drivers. And none of us will ever forget the day he stopped the race during the Italian Grand Prix at Monza, to try and pull his fellow racer Ronnie Peterson from the blazing cockpit of his car, single-handed. The man worked hard, and played harder dying prematurely in his Wimbledon home in 1993, at the age of just forty five. A truly sad end to one of Britain's greatest, most charismatic, formula one racing legends who only saw the need to become world champion once and once only.

Ilie Nastase was a true sporting legend, the darling of the tennis world. With his dark smoldering looks, long black hair, fiery Rumanian temperament, natural ability and infectious charisma. Ilie possessed every conceivable shot as laid out in the tennis manual, and then some. Making the impossible appear effortless and simplistic in the heat of battle on Wimbledon's hallowed centre court. Seventies tennis was glamorous and exciting with thanks to gifted gladiators like: the 'tough street fighter' Jimmy Connors, the 'ice cold Swede' Bjorn Borg and Arthur Ashe. Locked in tense, nail biting encounters, sometimes lasting for hours before the game was won. In the summer of 1973, Ilie Nastase came to Wimbledon to win the one missing jewel in his crown having reached the top spot in the tennis world, and hotly tipped to become the new champion. As expected, he made it through to the final fairly easily to face former American serviceman Stan Smith, in one of the greatest centre court battles in the history of the game. Ilie dominated much of the game and was balanced on match point when somehow Stan Smith fought back, clawing himself out of the quagmire he was trapped in, to eventually win the match and deprive Ilie Nastase of the best chance he was ever going to have to win Wimbledon. A second centre court final turned out to be a disaster for Ilie, going out in straight sets to Bjorn Borg, who went on to win Wimbledon six times. A day when Ilie Nastase allowed his many tangled emotional demons to get the better of him, his Achilles Heel, which prevented him from claiming the one trophy he longed to win so badly, but never did.

On a perfect day firing on all six cylinders and armed with an awesome spontaneous repertoire of shots, Ilie Nastase was untouchable. But on another day, when the demons were running loose inside his head spoiling his sporting prowess, he became an entirely different creature. Volatile, angry, desperate, uncoordinated eyes darkening as the match slipped beyond his reach, causing him to fly into uncontrollable rages; his mood permeating every nook and cranny of centre court. That said, balancing out the good with the bad, he was the one tennis player who loved to perform for the people watching him. Small wonder they flocked to watch him, hoping to be entertained regardless of the outcome. A common attribute George Best, Ilie Nastase and James Hunt each shared. Allowing them to go out and play the game, the way they wanted to play it.

As Bob and I stood with the mourners on that cold, wet, rainy, sad day, watching George Best's coffin inch its way over to Roselawn cemetery, he pointed out to me a large, gold, silken flag tied to a lamppost featuring a white shield with a red hand. He explained to me that it was the flag of Ulster, representing hundreds of years' of history and heritage. Ulster being one of the four main provinces making up Northern Ireland, the hand in turn, representing the symbol of the O'Neill clan, who were one of the strongest, fiercest ruling clans at the time. One of Belfast's citizens' had written a black felt pen message on the flag, serving as the perfect tribute to George Best. A person who'd gone to a lot of thought to have come up with such a clear, concise, sentiment that to me said it all, and then some about the lives and skills of three of the world's greatest footballers' all who played 'the beautiful game', their way. Summed up perfectly in six words which read: Maradona, Good – Pele, Better - George Best!

NINE

Diego Maradona was born in Argentina in October 1960. During his often controversial twenty one-year football career, he made a total of four hundred and ninety one club appearances coupled with ninety-one national appearances, scoring two hundred and fifty nine goals and thirty-four goals respectively. His appearance wasn't exactly your stereotypical footballers' image. He was short and stocky, barrel chested with thick muscular tree trunk legs and shaggy black hair. Who was loved and adored by millions of fans the world over, who nicknamed him 'Dios', which was a mix up of his playing number and the Spanish word for God.

A journalist with the Houston Chronicle once wrote the following words about the bandy legged striker. 'To understand the gargantuan shadow Maradona casts over his football mad homeland, one has to conjure up the athleticism of Michael Jordan, the power of Babe Ruth and the human fallibility of Mike Tyson in a single person, and there you have Diego Maradona.' During the 1986 World Cup tournament Maradona exploded onto the international footballing world with a vengeance, becoming a vital part of the Argentinean team that went on to win the Jules Rimet trophy. But it was during the Argentina vs England game that he really did hit the spotlight, for two very different reasons!

As Argentina attacked the English goalmouth, a ball is sent into the area causing Maradona to go for it. Rising high above the England keeper, he knocked the ball into the back of the net with his hand! A very unsporting moment he will be associated with forever. Adding insult to injury he dubbed the goal as 'The Hand of God.' Despite this most outrageous moment he went on to redeem himself with the little matter of his second goal in the same game; a goal which was voted as the goal of the century by FIFA in 2002. It was a moment of unmistakable sheer brilliance when he picked up the ball in his own half and set off towards the England goal mouth. A magical, weaving, darting, perfectly balanced run covering almost the length of the field, in only eleven moves, shunning all attempts to get him off the ball, before placing the ball in the net. A goal it has to be noted was scored during Maradona's well publicised seventeen year battle with a cocaine addiction, eventually ending his playing career with Napoli on the island of Sicily. Where even today, Diego Maradona is revered as a God, and shrines to his memory are tended to with loving care and attention.

Born in Brazil, in October 1940, Edson Arantes De Nascimento, his parents naming him after the American inventor Thomas Edison, is the name given to the man who the world knew simply as Pele. As a player he broke every record going before rising to the lofty position of footballing ambassador. His name forever associated with every aspect of 'the beautiful game.'
In his twenty one year career Pele appeared in over one thousand three hundred games, in which he knocked up a tally of one thousand two hundred and eighty one goals. He remains to this day Brazil's top scorer, with seventy two goals in ninety two national appearances, and remains along side West German legend Uwe Seeler, as the only two players to have scored goals in four successive world cups.

Pele played a major role in Brazil winning the World Cup in Mexico in 1970. The true kings of South American Samba football were simply unbeatable in every way, through scintillating performances from the men in yellow, sky blue and white. Giving the world a breathtaking lesson in how to play 'the beautiful game' Copacabana style. He was 'the' legend in a team of eleven who will go down in history as 'the greatest football team ever.' Andy Warhol said of Pele 'He was one of the few people who contradicted my theory, instead of fifteen minutes of fame, he will have fifteen centuries.'

The very same legendary Pele who once commented when asked 'If he regarded himself as the world's best greatest footballer?' That in fact 'The Manchester United player George Best was in his opinion, the best player at the time.'

Born in Belfast, in May 1945, George Best's football career spanned some ten years from 1963 to 1973, in which he made four hundred and seventy four appearances for Manchester United, scoring a total of one hundred and eighty one goals, together with an international career for Northern Ireland. He was capped thirty seven times scoring nine goals, including the time he spent playing in America where he scored many sensational goals; including what many purport to be his all time greatest playing for San Jose Earthquakes. When he tore apart the Fort Lauderdale defence with a bewildering 'out of this world' run, beating man after man, before slamming the ball in the back of the net. When asked 'If he considered it his greatest goal?' He shrugged it off in typical understated George Best style, saying 'That it would have been, if he'd have scored the goal as a United player in front of the mighty Stretford End.' For me personally, the less said about American football and the negative influence it's had on our national game the better. Yes the money players' can earn as they approach their sell by date can be phenomenal, and one cannot blame them for cashing in at the end of a relatively short sporting career. But for me, America remains the graveyard for some of our truly great exponents of 'the beautiful game.'

For all of us who were fortunate enough to see George Best play, he only ever had one real playing career and that was the decade he spent at Manchester United. During which time he played a monumental part in them winning the football league and European Cup in 1968, as well as George winning the coveted 'Golden Ball' trophy, being voted 'the international player of the year.' He was only twenty three years old the night United beat Benfica at Wembley, a personal highlight for him. On the verge of what everyone thought was going to be a glittering career both at club, and international level.

But things failed to turn out as expected, because he never repeated the kind of success he achieved on that glorious night with United ever again. Nor did he achieve the kind of international success he longed for, wearing the dazzling emerald green of Northern Ireland. Every game he gave one hundred percent. He was far and above the best Irish player ever seen. While the rest of his team mates' appeared lacklustre in comparison, unable to keep up with his vision and talent, and one man cannot go out and win a game alone; a tragedy for world football, because George never really got the chance to play in a World Cup competition.

Despite this, he never spoke about his team mates' in a negative way and always professed that he was fiercely proud of his Northern Irish heritage and didn't want it any other way. I missed out on the earlier part of his career, only ever able to watch him on television; which is no substitute for the real thing.

Even so, the final three seasons he played for United in the early 70's, when his career and fitness were noticeably deteriorating, he still proved on countless occasions that he still possessed the flashes of talent, balance, shooting and dribbling ability the old George had in abundance, scoring so many goals during that time that many today regard as his finest ever. The memorable goal against Chelsea when he took the Blues on alone and still scored. His double hat-trick against lowly Northampton Town, in a game that despite being banned for four months, he showed he still had the skill to find the back of the net six times. A stunning goal from nowhere against West Ham, jumping on the slightest of chances in a busy penalty area slamming the ball home hard with killer precision, all the while being off balance and on the back foot. The day at Southampton when he smashed the 'scummers' to bits with a storming hat trick, and for many, arguably his greatest, in a sunny Old Trafford against Sheffield United. George on another jinking, dazzling solo attack on the Sheffield goal, whose defenders' assumed that he'd run out of steam and played himself into what looked like an impossible situation, then mere moments later he's standing there, arm raised, smiling after looping the ball into the back of the net from nowhere again. 'The Belfast Boy' in his declining years, but leaving me with so many magical memories that still bring a smile to my face when I'm enjoying a few clips of him on You-Tube.

In my opinion, out of all the truly great players' who've played for Manchester United, there have only been two who were born to play for the team, both who, if they'd had the choice, would still to this day have been a part of the structure in some way or another after their playing careers ended. One of these is David Beckham; who loved United throughout his career, and still does; and the other is George Best; whose only dream was to become a United player under the leadership of Sir Matt 'The Boss' Busby. George was one of the new Busby babes born out of the terrible tragedy of Munich. A Busby player who took it bad when he resigned, leaving the club and players to deal with the likes of Wilf McGuinness, Frank O'Farrell and Tommy Docherty; whom George hated with a passion, who just happened to be the man in charge when George finally left Manchester United forever at the end of the 73-74 season.

Just as he'd arrived at Old Trafford in 1961, George Best departed largely unannounced; never to wear the famed number seven shirt again. In a glittering, painfully prematurely ended career at Old Trafford, he'd made a fortune for the club, just because of who he was, and what he could do with a football. People came to watch him purely for the love of football, and his was a sizeable contribution to the Reds winning the league, FA Cup, and European Cup back in 1968. You would assume that because of this, and the ten years he gave himself to the club, that Manchester United would have rightfully awarded him a testimonial game, like they did for Denis Law and Bobby Charlton. Sadly, what could have been a fantastic night for George, and all the fans to say thanks and to wish each other well for the future, never materialised. The United board of directors had decided that for a player to earn the right to a testimonial, he had to have played a certain quota of games for the club. And George's appearance record fell short of the mark, despite his four hundred and seventy four appearances, scoring one hundred and eighty one goals!

That's the one thing I'll never be able to forgive Manchester United for. He should have been given a testimonial to send him on, to his future, in the correct way. Fortunately the Northern Irish F.A. stepped up and somewhat belatedly in 1988 organised a testimonial at Windsor Park, away from the politics and business of Old Trafford. In front of a packed crowd and dignitaries such as Sir Matt Busby and Bob Bishop, the scout who discovered the boy-genius, Best scored twice.

Three years later, I was fortunate to watch the closest equivalent to a George Best testimonial game I was ever going to see, with George in his near-prime. It was during the 76-77 season when George found himself playing football for Fulham; who were due to play a fixture against Blackpool at Bloomfield Road. A gorgeous sunny day at the seaside, with the ground busier than it had been in ages, due no doubt to everyone wanting to watch George Best alongside another fantastic player 'back in the day', the one and only Rodney Marsh. The game turned out to be a wonderful light hearted affair, dominated by Best and Marsh, who looked to be enjoying themselves throughout the game; messing about like two kids having a kick about, playfully tackling and fouling each other to the crowds' amusement. The very last time I watched George Best for real and still holding the same smile on my face I had after watching him the first time. And it doesn't get better than that!

So in the final analysis of the time honoured argument as to who is the better of the three players highlighted on the Ulster flag draped above all our heads on that dreadfully sad morning? The facts speak for themselves.

Pele enjoyed a long, spectacular, unblemished career, whereas Diego Maradona and George Best fell victim to their own personal demons. Pele and Maradona enjoyed the kind of glittering international careers George Best was deprived of, through no fault of his own so its fair to assume that on that aspect alone, Pele and Maradona have the edge over him, but when it comes down to club level there is nothing separating all three in terms of skill and match winning capability. At the end of the day it all comes down to personal choice in answering the one question 'Who was the greatest footballer ever?' A balancing act caught between cold, clear facts and heartfelt emotions.

For me the answer is found in the magical moment combining all the skill, vision and ability needed to turn a lost game into a victory. With time running out, the packed Old Trafford faithful angry and frustrated at United being a goal down to a team they should be destroying, when George Best decides enough is enough! The ball became his own personal property, picked up deep inside the United half, as he sets off on one of his typical runs. Providing a sudden surge of hope, where seconds before there was none. Past one defender, and another, the perfect dummy, a swivel of the hips, passing the ball between the defender's legs leaving him snarling with embarrassment and George is gone en route to the goal mouth below the Stretford End; then a neat precise, one-two, with Kidd, Charlton or Law. The return pass pitched perfectly onto the end of his boot, gliding past two more defenders like the Marie Celeste, their despairing attempts to foul him amounting to nothing as he surges towards the goal. The keeper stands there nervously knowing what is to come, wondering where George is going to place the ball, anxiously jumping up and down on the spot, left, right, left, right trying to read, the unreadable in George's inscrutable eyes and mercurial feet. Its 'now or never', ' do or die' stuff, as the goalie makes his move, a dive to the left totally falling for the feint in George's body language as the ball slides past him into the back of the net! United are back in the game thanks to the 'Belfast Boy' who stands there arm aloft, triumphant; the inevitable 'I told you so' smile on his face, drinking in the moment, soaking up the thunderous applause.

During those spontaneous magical moments he effortlessly conjured up week in, week out, in grounds all over the country I seriously dare you to think of another player that can even come close to playing every defensive and attacking aspect of 'the beautiful game' the way George Best played it? Go on, I dare you.

LAST ORDERS

Alcohol. We can buy the stuff just about anywhere these days. It's even on sale in garage shops tempting motorists to grab a bottle of their favourite tipple while queuing to pay for their petrol. Along with the tobacco industry, it's a government approved industry earning them millions in tax that costs society in general over two hundred billion pounds a year. The NHS some three and a half million pounds while eleven million is spent on alcohol related crimes and over seven billion in lost productivity.

Far from me sounding harsh and uncaring, a large part of me breathed a huge sigh of relief as my partner Karen died in the early hours of the morning after losing her lifetime battle against the booze. A tragic ending to a stormy frequently insane eight year roller coaster relationship we shared that began innocently enough with a cheap bottle of Dupre Brandy and ended with me drowning my sorrows shortly after she died with a bottle of Glenlivet Malt. A kaleidoscope of so many memories flooding through me from Goa to Moscow, Spain to Ireland as if I was sitting solo in my own private cinema watching a film about two people in their forties who unexpectedly fell in love one sunny morning. Each of us bringing along our own emotional baggage as we set out on a journey together hoping to chance upon some happiness and optimism we never managed to find.

Karen died almost five years to the day when a young doctor in Galway hospital told her in no uncertain terms to quit the booze or else she would die. A warning that went in one ear and out of the other sitting in the Spanish Arch half an hour later watching her swallow a large brandy down in one laughing away as she tried to convince me that the doctor was wrong in his diagnosis that she wasn't even close to being an alcoholic, a misguided belief she believed in right up until the bitter end. A beautiful broken doll of a woman who often confessed to me that she had her first drink at the age of twelve and had been pissed ever since. Booze became her own private refuge, a place where she found fleeting comfort and happiness far removed from the increasing pain and suffering she suffered in the real world. The reasons why she drank so much because of the horrific childhood experiences no little girl should have to go trough that will remain with me forever.

I've known a number of alcoholics over the years and in my experience they all drank simply to forget the past. I can well understand Karen's need for getting out of her head as much as she did but what need did George Best have to allow his addiction to booze to manifest to the point where it destroyed his career and his life in such a painful horrible way? I've watched George Best from a child to a man both on and off the field since he captivated my attention with his unique charisma and talent that were responsible for him becoming one of the greatest footballers of all time and to me there were always two very opposite George Bests living within the same body as there was with Karen who could light up a room the second she walked in and hours later, be lying there on the floor a broken doll wrapped around a bottle of booze.

On the field George Best was the undisputed king of all he surveyed, confident, aggressive, cocky, charismatic, spontaneous when he needed to be and both the crowd and himself knew it. He was completely at home with himself on the football field and this reflected in the way he played the game he loved. We all knew that from the second he walked out on to the pitch, something magical almost beyond belief could happen but off the field I always felt that he was never at his best; that things were always out of his control. The young timid lad from Belfast who arrived on the scene unnoticed before blossoming into the worlds first global superstar appeared to be nothing like the mop haired flash of genius in the crimson number seven shirt making compete fools of any opposition. He advertised everything from aftershave, football boots to sausages and made fortunes from it. To me though, he always appeared awkward, apprehensive; like a fish out of water allowing the advertising men to sell his sex appeal and charisma. In the end it took precedence over the awesome natural talent he was born with. As a result I feel he continually struggled to perfect the public persona the media demanded from him.

Over the years many people (so called) 'close to George' have cited various reasons responsible for him drinking to excess. Loneliness, a need for company, to be liked and the fact that his football career peaked far too early having won virtually everything a player can win by the age of twenty three. From scoring a brilliant goal against Benfica helping his beloved Manchester United to become the first English club to win the European Cup on that glorious action packed Wembley night in 1968. George went from that incredible sporting pinnacle to winning nothing again. Perhaps a strong enough reason as the painful reality kicked in that he was never going to equal that again to hit the bottle in an attempt to numb the pain and frustration of sporting underachievement. I don't know but people react to failure in so many different ways and maybe this was the reason why George Best sought comfort in the bottle.

For me, and I suspect for many people out there who admired and cared about him, his tragic appearance on the Terry Wogan show, clearly drunk, eyes glazed over trying to match Terry word for word, laughing at his own jokes thinking he was being humorous, entertaining when in reality he was anything but was truly one of the saddest moments to witness from a player who had the world at his feet.

We're all different to one another when it comes down to the way we live our lives, how many of us destroy ourselves with drink and drugs. You don't have to famous to be an alcoholic lying on your death bed, body jaundiced, emaciated, stomach swollen iron hard connected to a colostomy bag waiting for death 'to take me to a better place Pete' as Karen told me shortly before she died. From the many accounts I've read about George Bests final few hours alive and watching Karen die a similar death caused by identical reasons. They both displayed remarkable courage when facing death blaming nobody but themselves for the tragic way they ruined their lives. The brave message George wrote and displayed on his death proclaimed 'Do Not Die Like Me'.

In the grounds of Lancaster's Royal Infirmary one evening talking together, Karen told me that if she could have a final wish. It would be to make a full on documentary of the ten painful days she spent in hospital before she died in the hope that it would serve as a warning to others. Sadly that never happened but there is a documentary in my head I've watched over and over again and believe me. Dying of acute alcoholic poisoning is a hideous, agonising, undignified end so many people assume will never happen to them as another double vodka or brandy goes down in one with a hearty 'cheers'.

LEGACY

Eight years ago George Best's sister Barbara gave up full time work to create the George Best Foundation with the aim of helping sportsmen suffering from alcohol problems come to terms with their illness and try to beat it. Over the years it has donated over two hundred and eighty thousand pounds to various sporting causes which is no mean achievement. Sadly due to increasing ill health, Barbara decided to call it a day in 2014 and close down the foundation but the essence of the charity lives on diverting all the monies remaining to worthwhile causes.

The George Best Trail was conceived by a group of Belfast charities to give visiting tourists and fans a taste of what it was like for the young George growing up in Belfast. The tiny family home at 16 Burren Way on the Cregagh estate is now a museum where fans can go and spend a weekend in the house where George spent his childhood. Complete with the original décor and the bed in which he slept as a youngster dreaming of 'fame and fortune.' Hosted by knowledgeable guides the walk takes you from his house to the school he attended, the playing fields where he first played football, the back alley where he spent so many hours knocking a ball against a wall, the cinema, the chippie where he used to buy his supper and the ice cream parlour he loved to hang out in. Then there's the Oval football ground, home to Glentoran FC where George watched countless matches as a child with his granddad dreaming of one day becoming the legend he was.

The grave in the neatly manicured tranquillity of Belfast's Roselawn Cemetery is the final poignant resting place for George Best who is buried alongside his mother in the family plot. A shiny black marble head stone covered in floral tributes, personal messages on cards and football scarves all around from just some of the people he touched. He, whose name will remain forever long after the likes of us have turned to dust leaving me wondering if there will ever be a day when a similar skinny young kid, all champagne eyes and cheeky smile, will come charging through the mist with the ball at his feet; bursting with enough talent and ambition to help him reach for the stars without having to rely on the likes of Big Brother and Britain's Got Talent to win his fortune and fame; dreaming that one day, through the love of the beautiful game, an ability to do magic with a football and sheer determination will one day perhaps be 'better than the Best'.

BY THE SAME AUTHOR

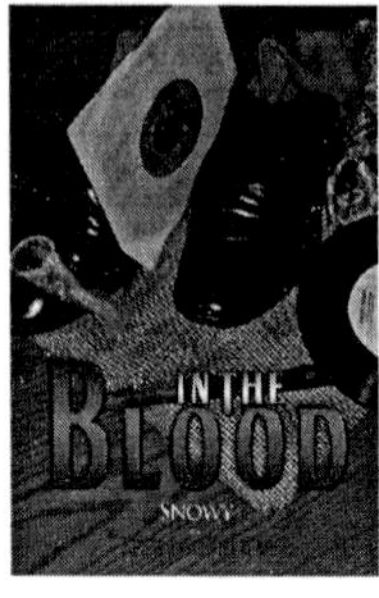

Pete McKenna is author of Nightshift, Who the Hells Frank Wilson and Maradona good; Pele better; GEORGE BEST. He is also co-author, along with Ian Snowball, of: In the Blood, Feed Your Head, All Souled Out, Tribes and The Teams That Dream in Caffs.

Available from all good books shops and Amazon.

Future books available soon include JERUSALEM, a hard hitting controversial semi fictional excursion into the moral and social decay of contemporary Britain, a country far removed from the once green and pleasant land of old; TINSELTOWN; a childhood memoir of growing up in the 60's and 70's during a time that can never be repeated, and a re-release of the cult classic WHO THE HELL'S FRANK WILSON, a fast paced, dark, stylish, violent romp set in 70's Blackpool mixing up Northern Soul with made-to-measure gangsters.

Other works in progress include AUTUMN LEAVES, an intriguing fictional novel about a haunted vintage tenor saxophone and the people who come into contact with it, and HOLOCAUST PAST TO PRESENT, a factual work on the chilling comparisons between the 67 year Jewish persecution of the Palestinians and the conduct of the Nazis as they carried out the Holocaust in the Second World War.